GYUTO

GYUTO

Monastic Life

Photographs by Tobi Wilkinson

Lustrum Press

*Nobody bestows enlightenment, no one owns it.
Fully realising your own nature is what Buddhas
call enlightenment.*

Sutra Of Condensed Perfect Qualities

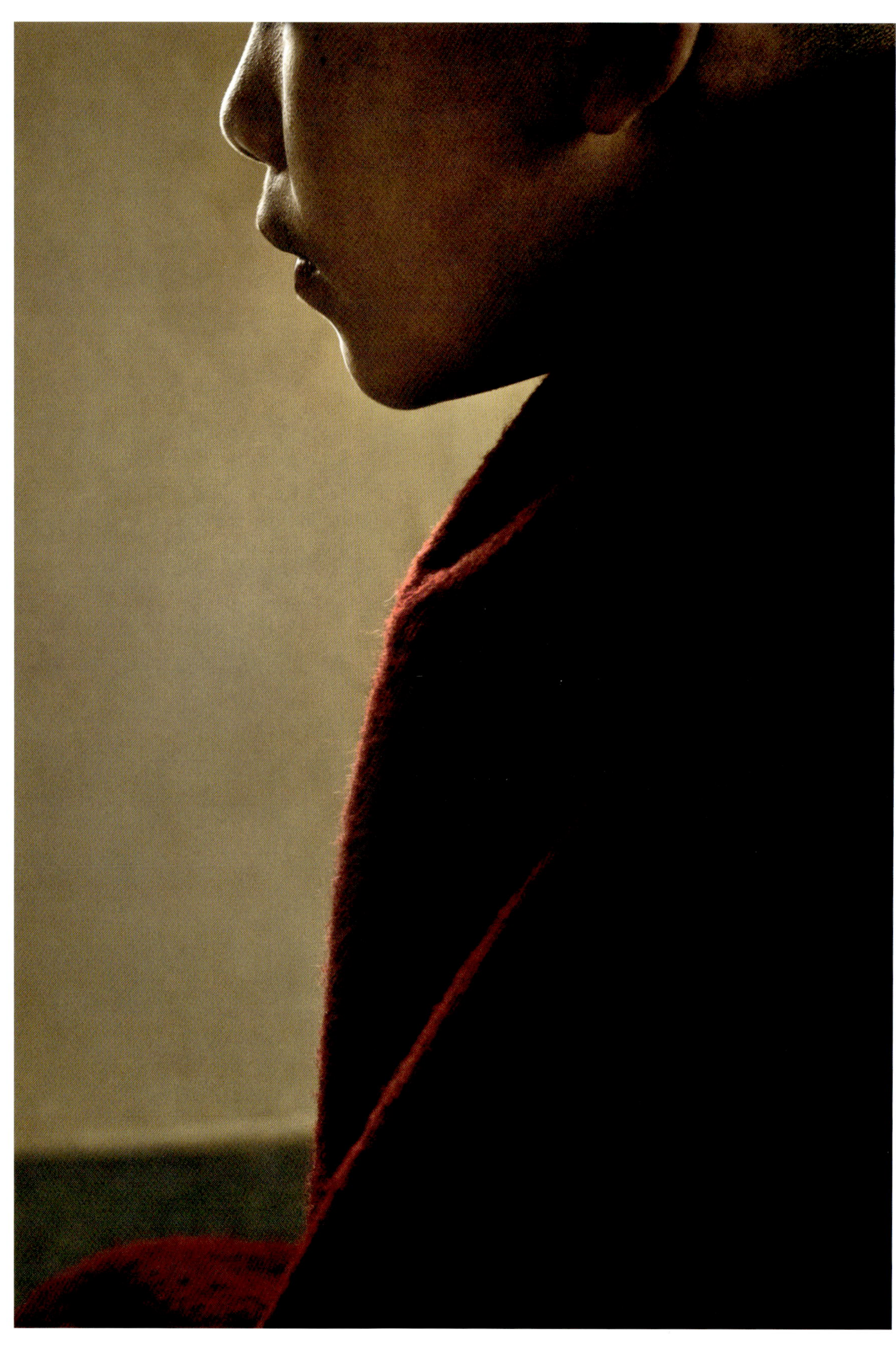

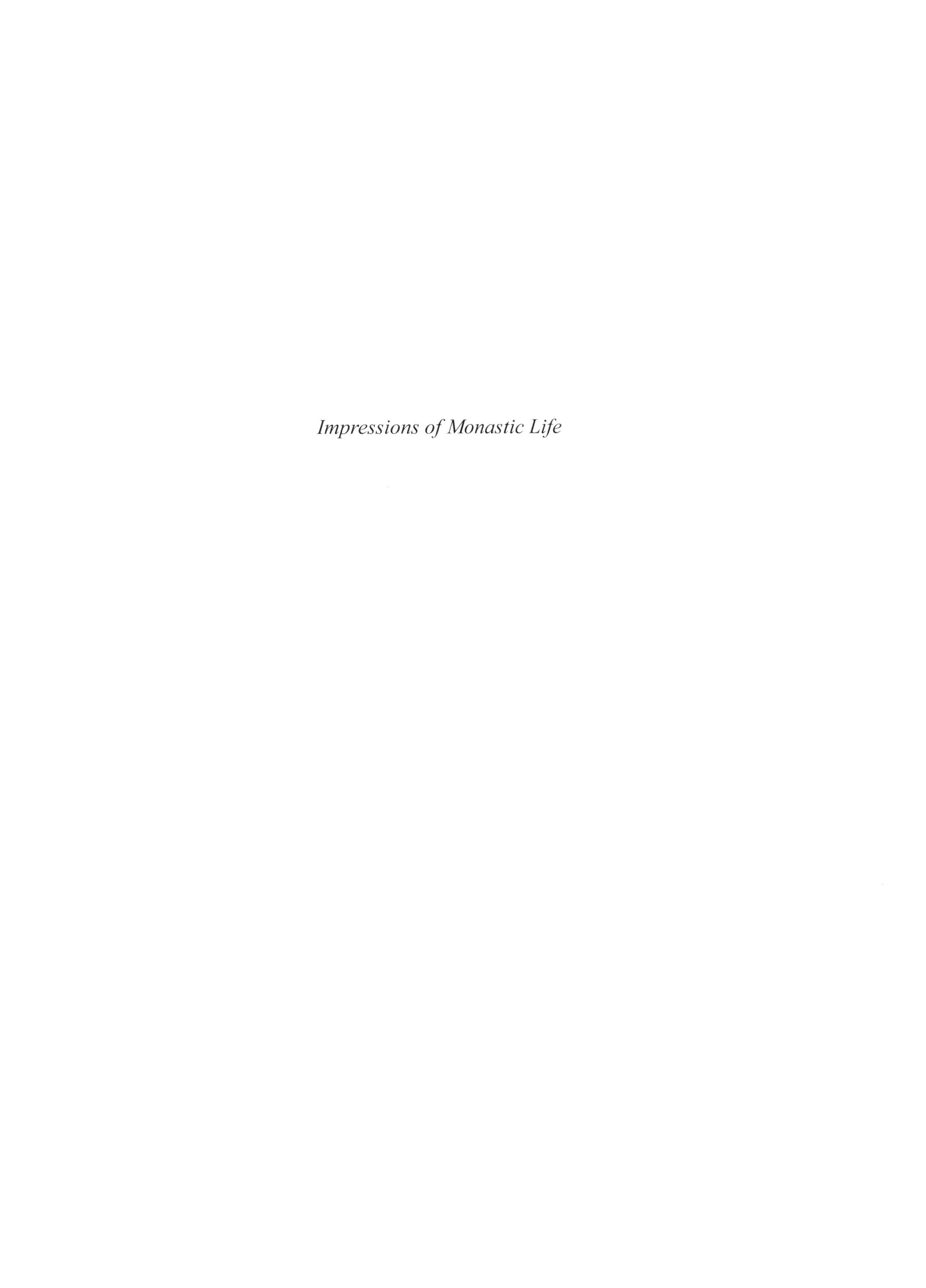

Impressions of Monastic Life

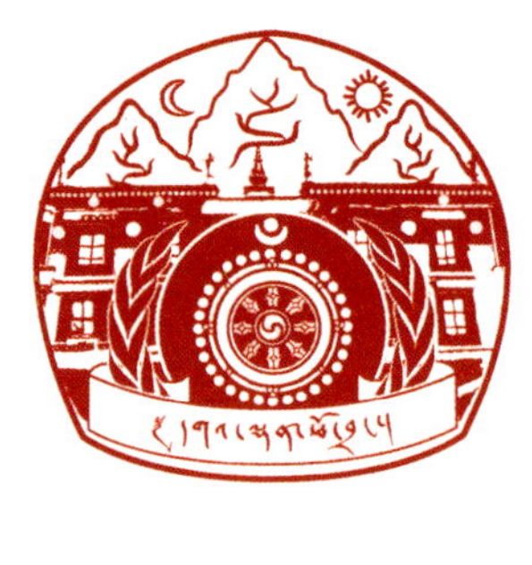

THE DALAI LAMA

MESSAGE

I welcome the publication of this book of photographs focusing on Gyuto Tantric College, which brings together views of the monastery campus as well as scenes from the life that goes on within.

Gyuto Monastery is a community of monks, individuals whose primary aim is to attain liberation and enlightenment. They seek to transform their minds by overcoming their disturbing emotions. While householders face many opportunities for disturbing emotions to grow, monks observe a discipline intended to lead to their reduction. Essentially, monks are free to do spiritual practice.

Like their brothers at Gyudmed Tantric College, the monks of Gyuto are well known for their strict discipline. Over the last 40 years or so in exile, they have also responded positively to my appeal to take up the study of the classic texts of Buddhist philosophy and epistemology.

In addition to that they have a special role within the Gelugpa Order of Tibetan Buddhism. At a certain point late in his life, Je Tsongkhapa, the founder of the Gelugpa Tradition asked his followers, "Who will be responsible for upholding my tantric tradition?" Jetsun Sherab Senge volunteered. He went on to found Gyudmed Tantric College. His disciple, Jetsun Kunga Dondrup, later founded Gyuto.

Thus, it has been the responsibility of the monks of these two monasteries down the centuries to maintain the purity of Tsongkhapa's tantric tradition through dedicated study and practice. This is reflected in the rule that candidates for Ganden Tripa, Holder of Je Tsongkhapa's Throne and Spiritual Head of the Gelugpa Order, must previously have served as Abbot of Gurne or Gyuto Tantric College.

I trust this book will serve to increase interested people's appreciation of the noble, centuries-old traditions that thrive today at Gyuto.

His Holiness 14th Dalia Lama

December 2nd, 2017

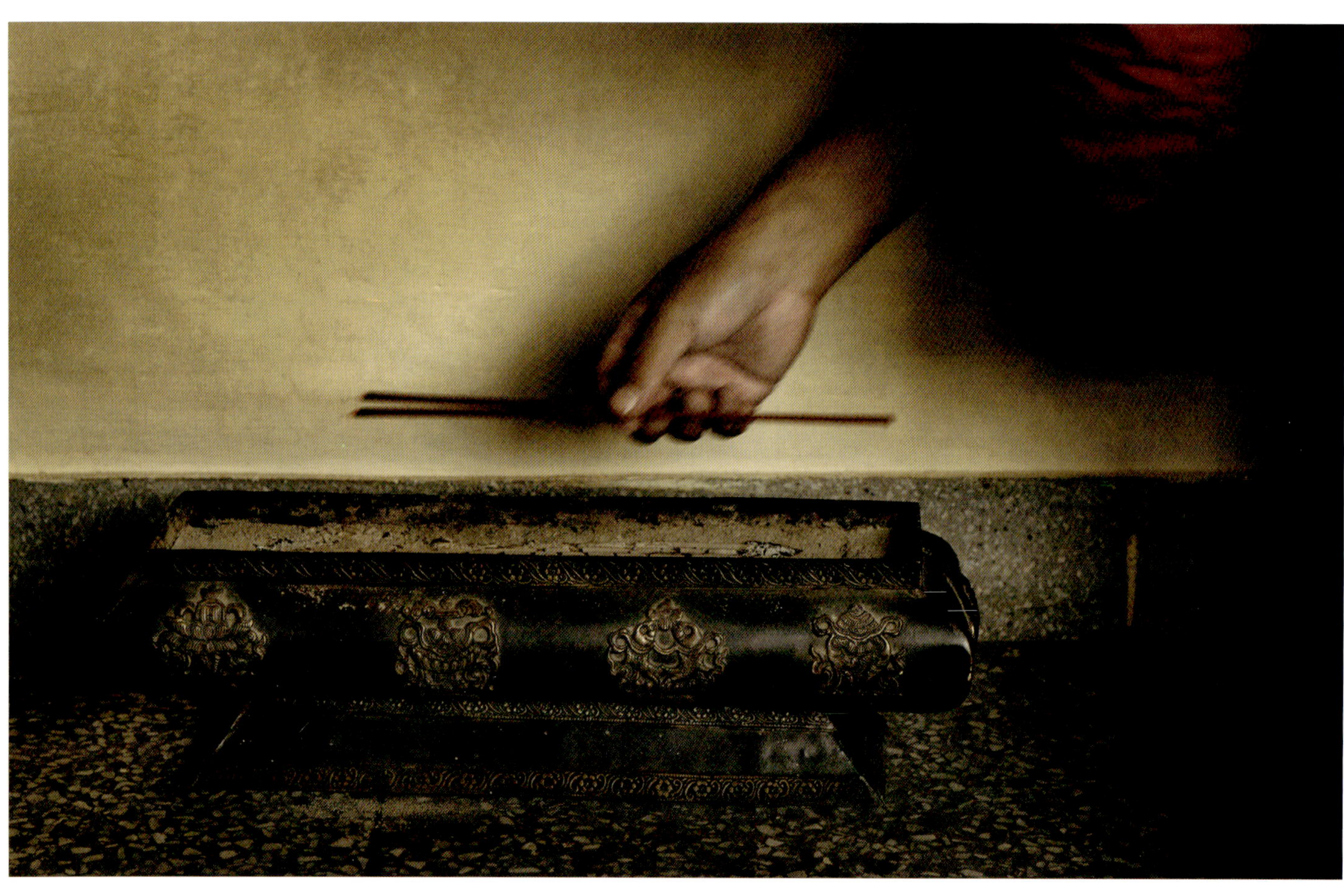

Nothing is random.

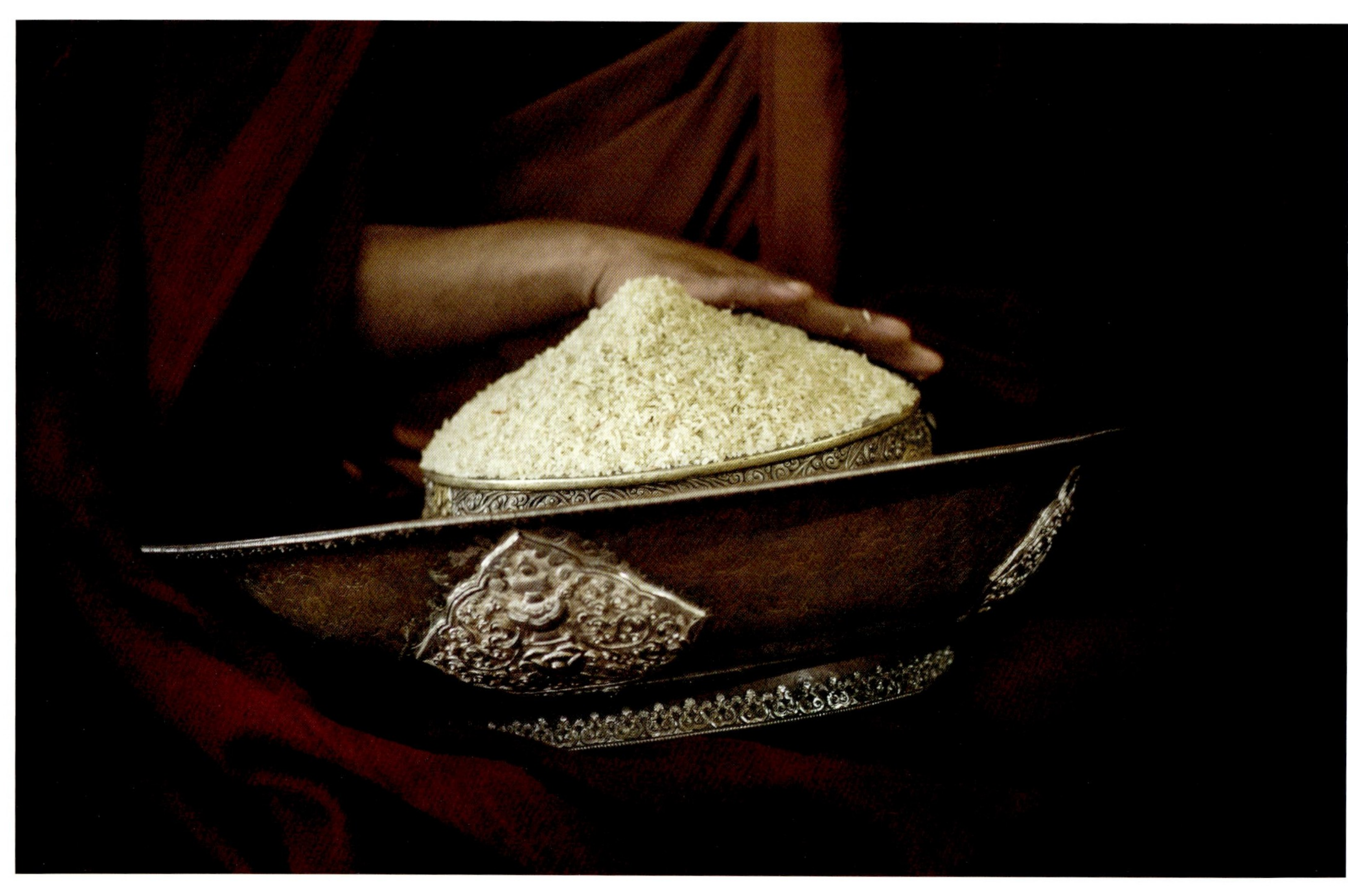

Compassion.

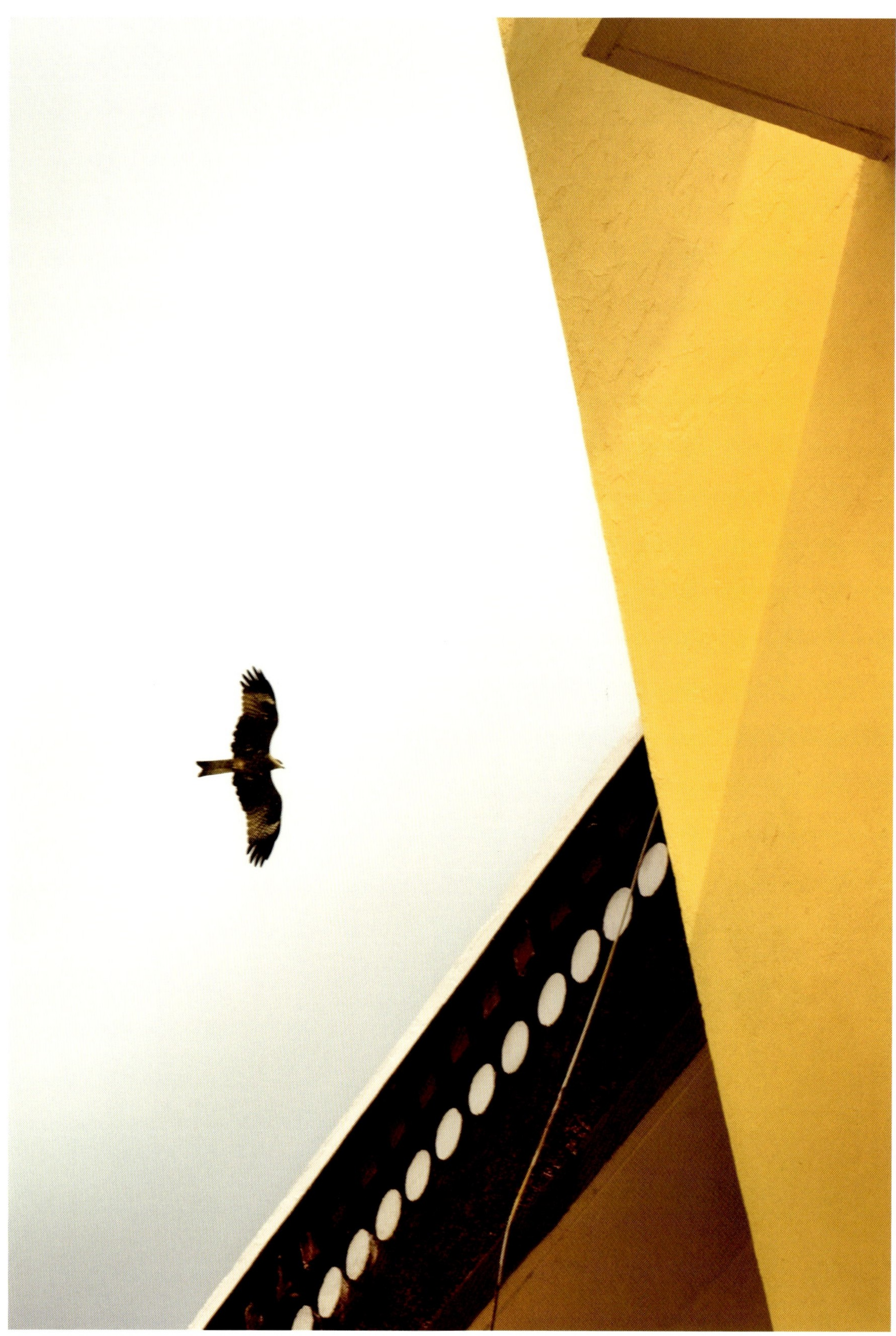

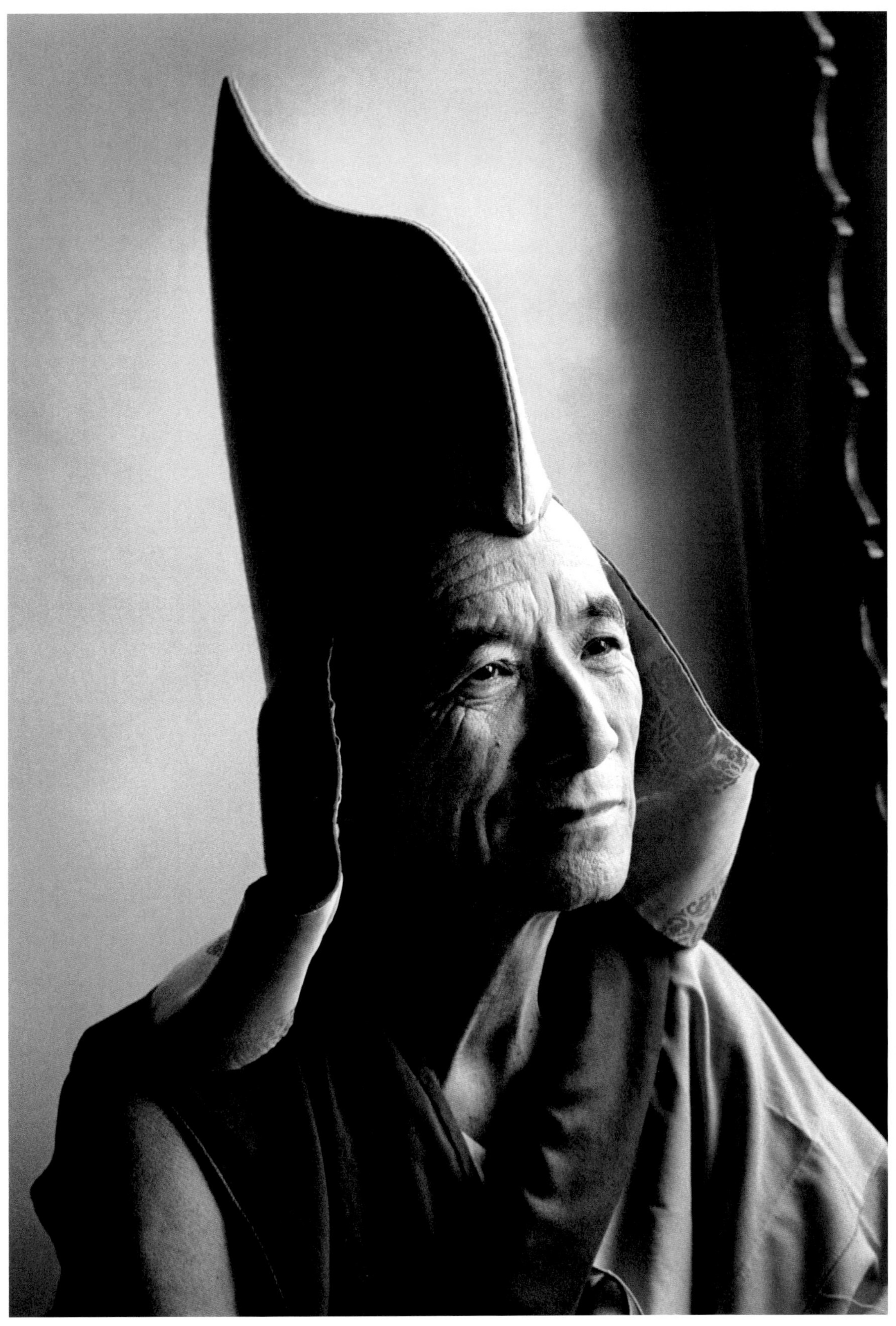

Everything is spiritual.

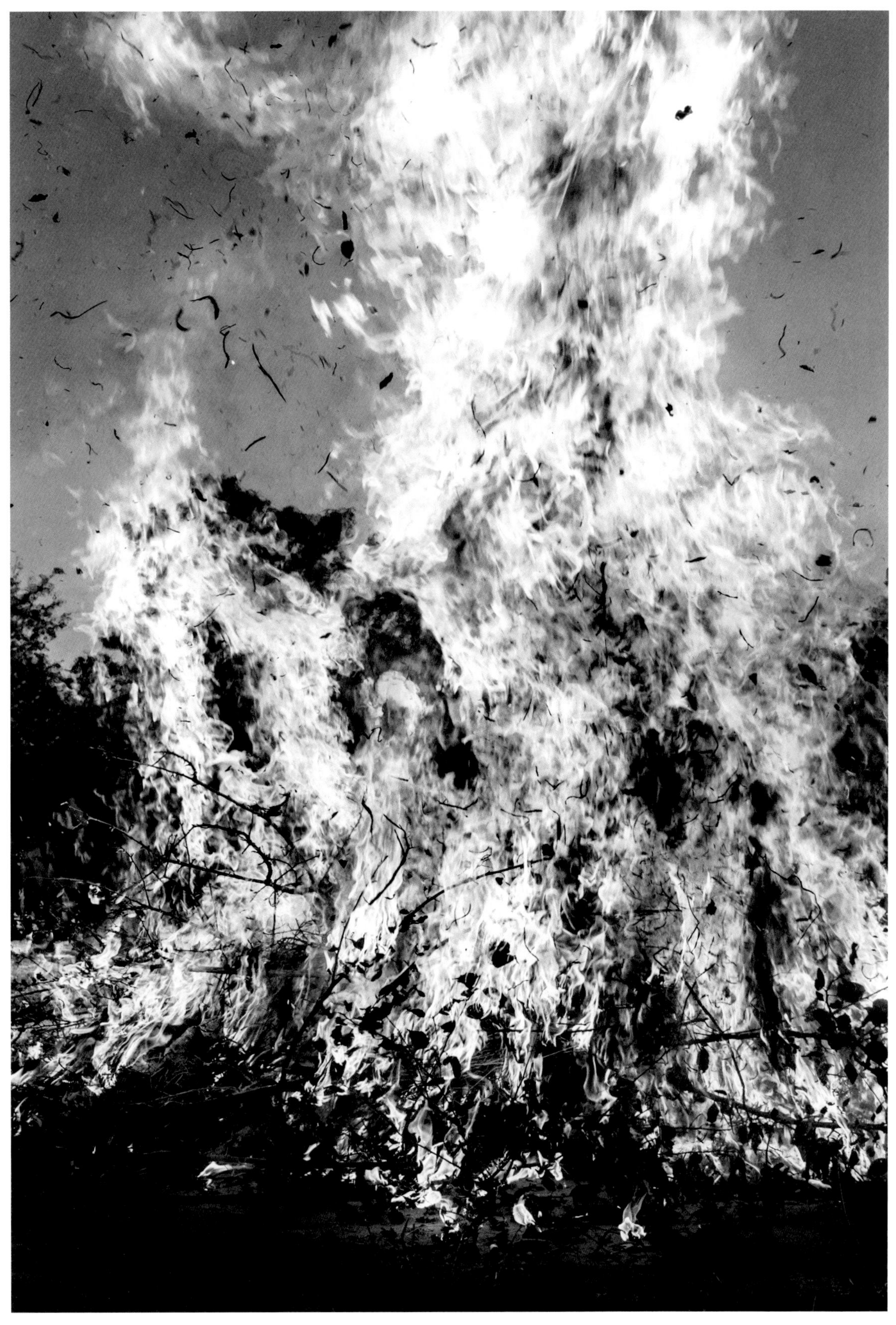

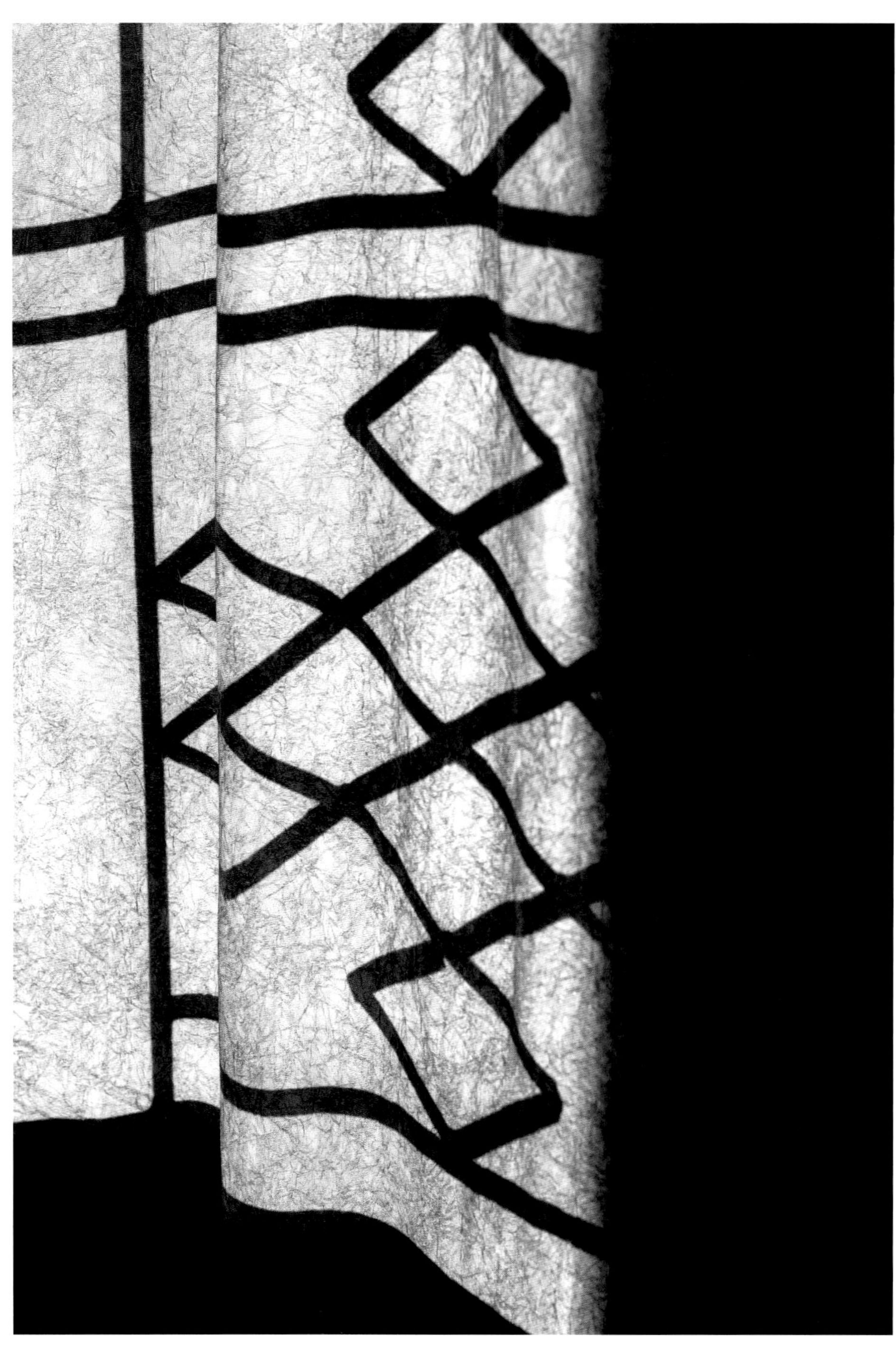

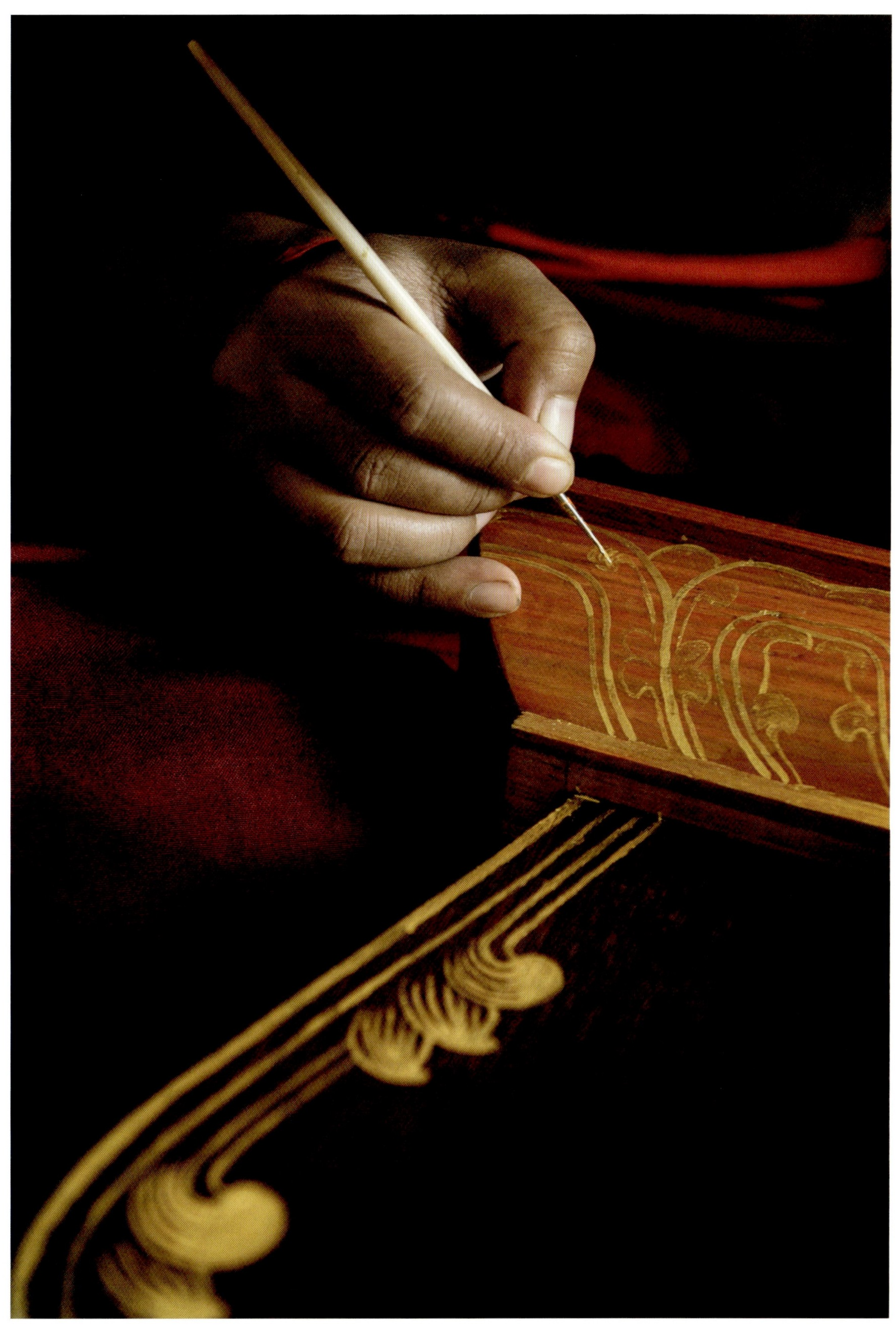

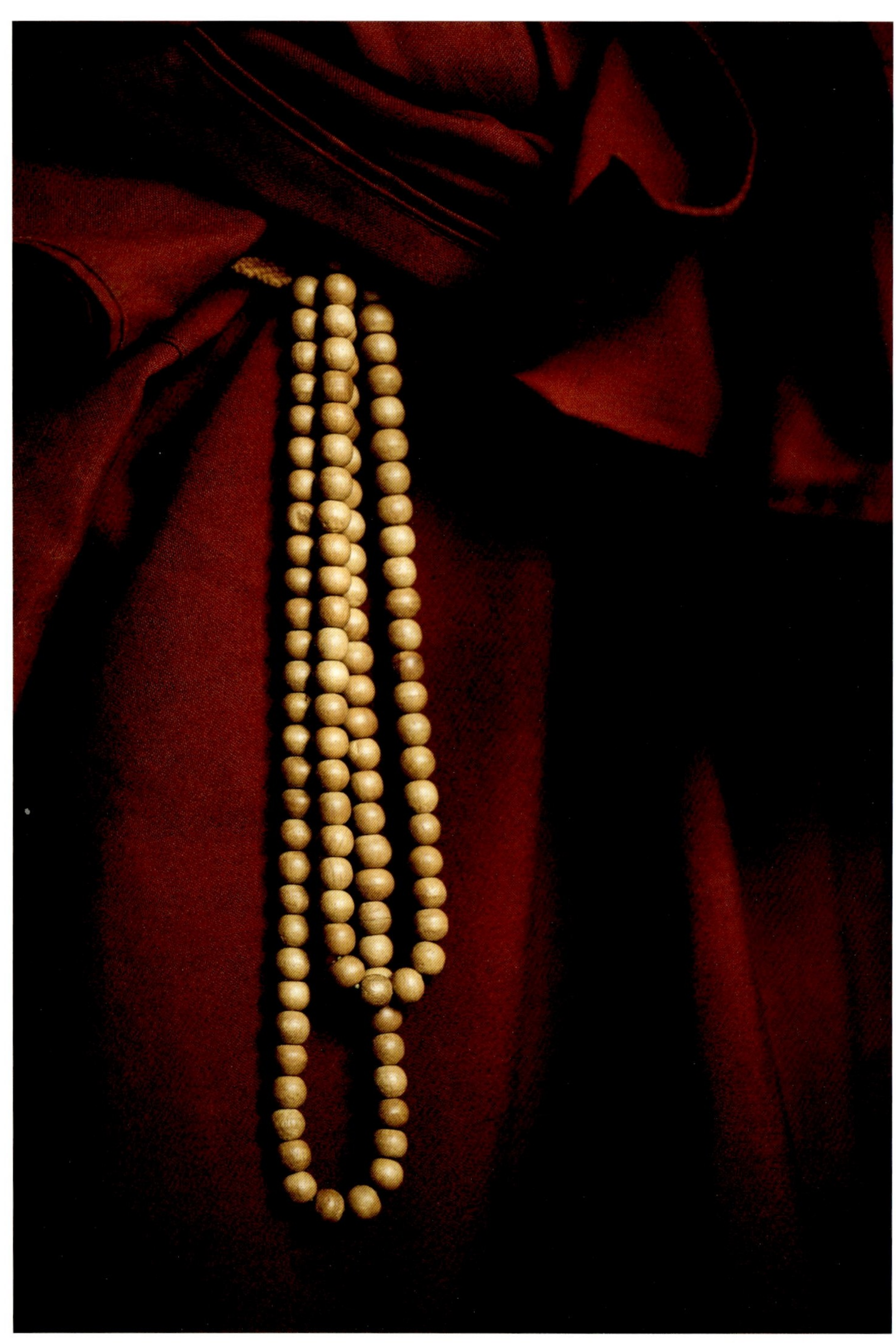

Permanency is an illusion.

Be gentle first with yourself.

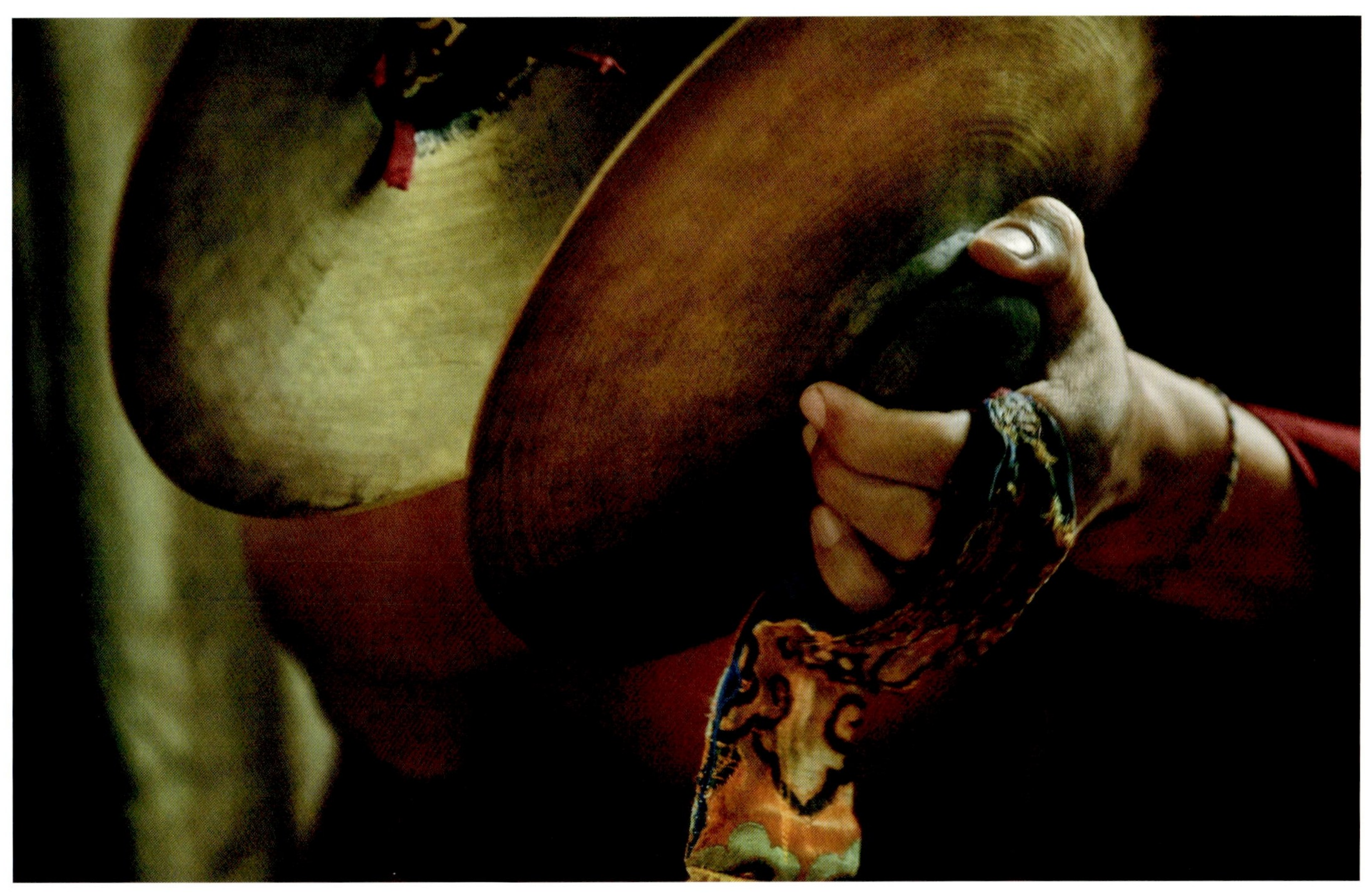

It is never too late.

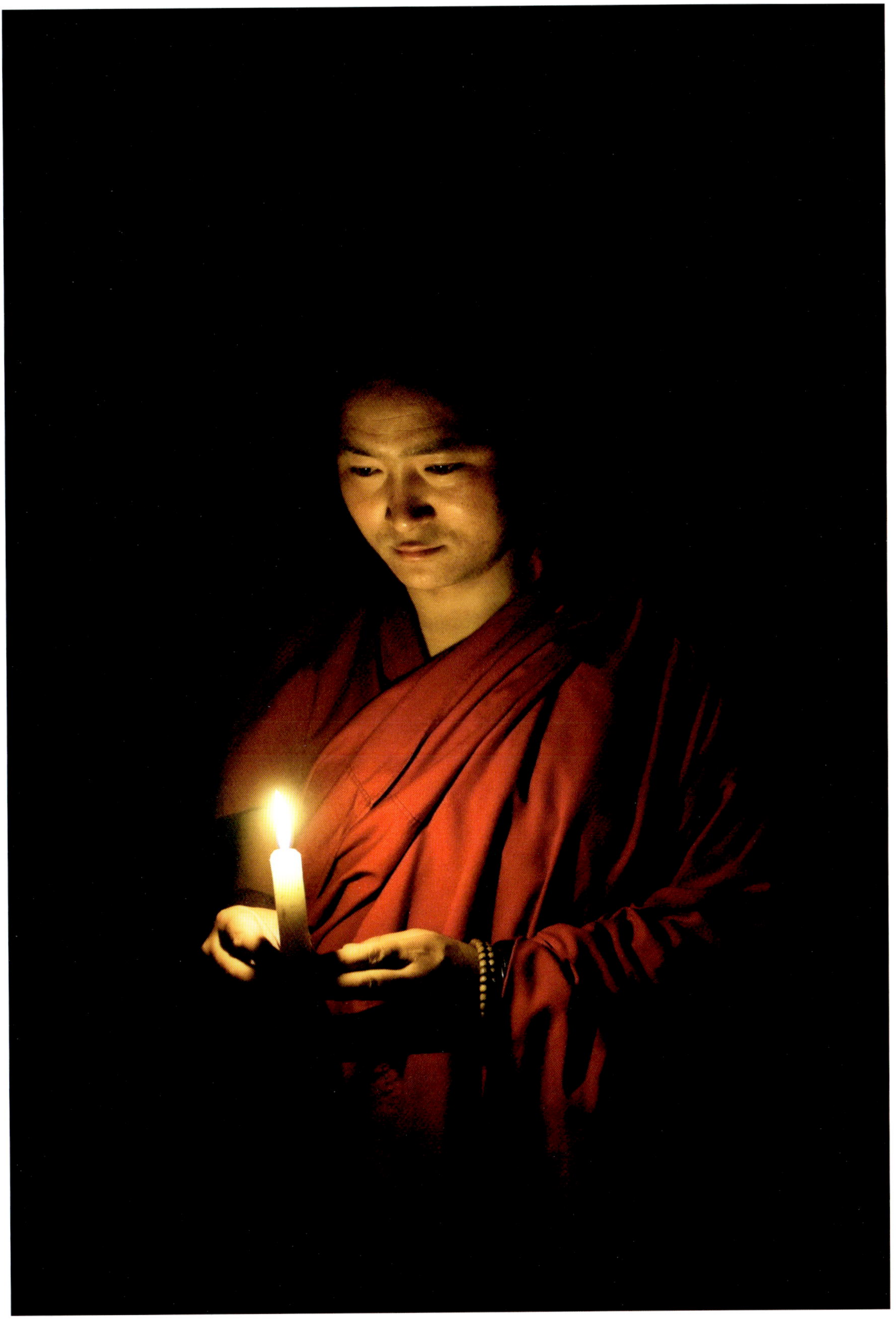

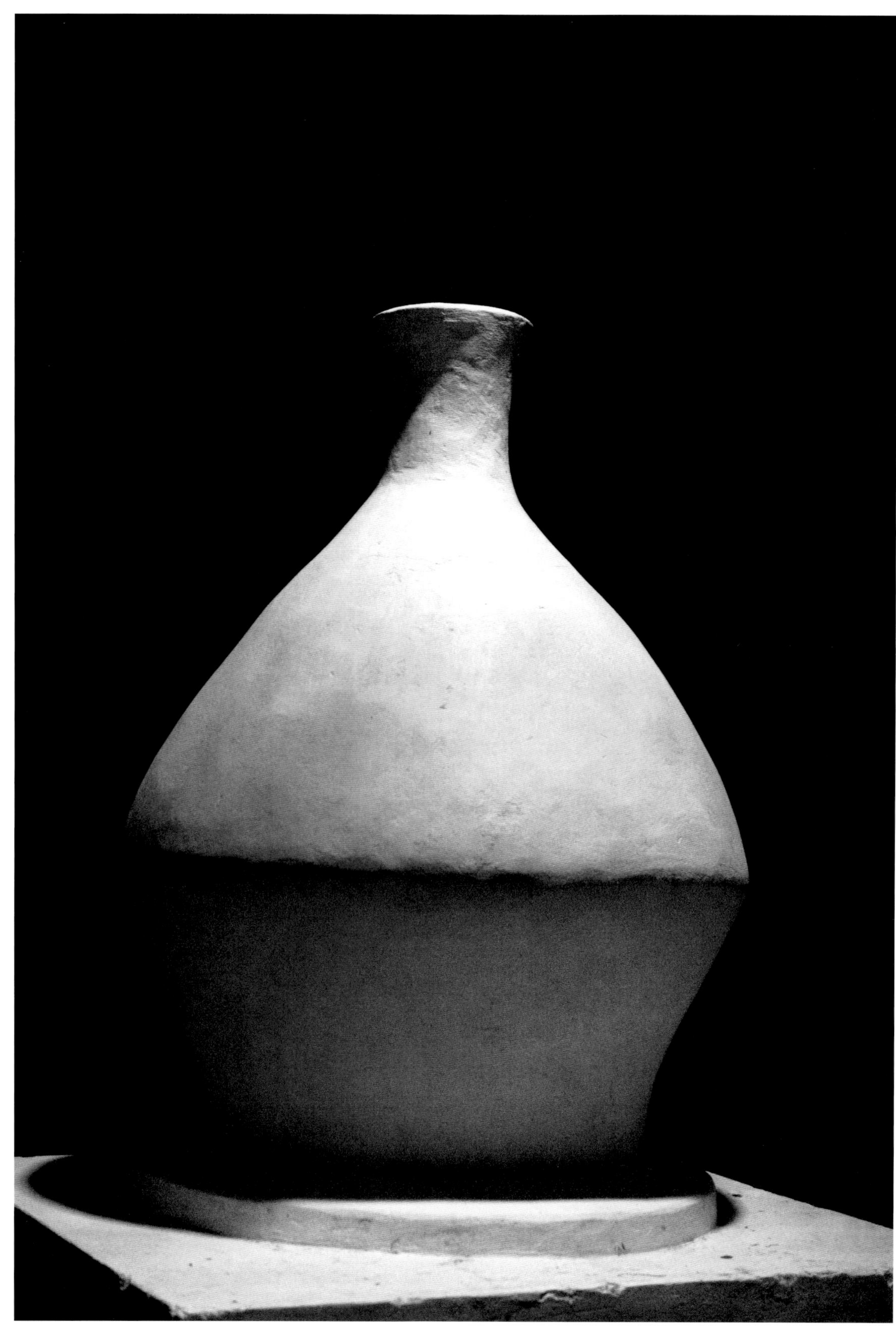

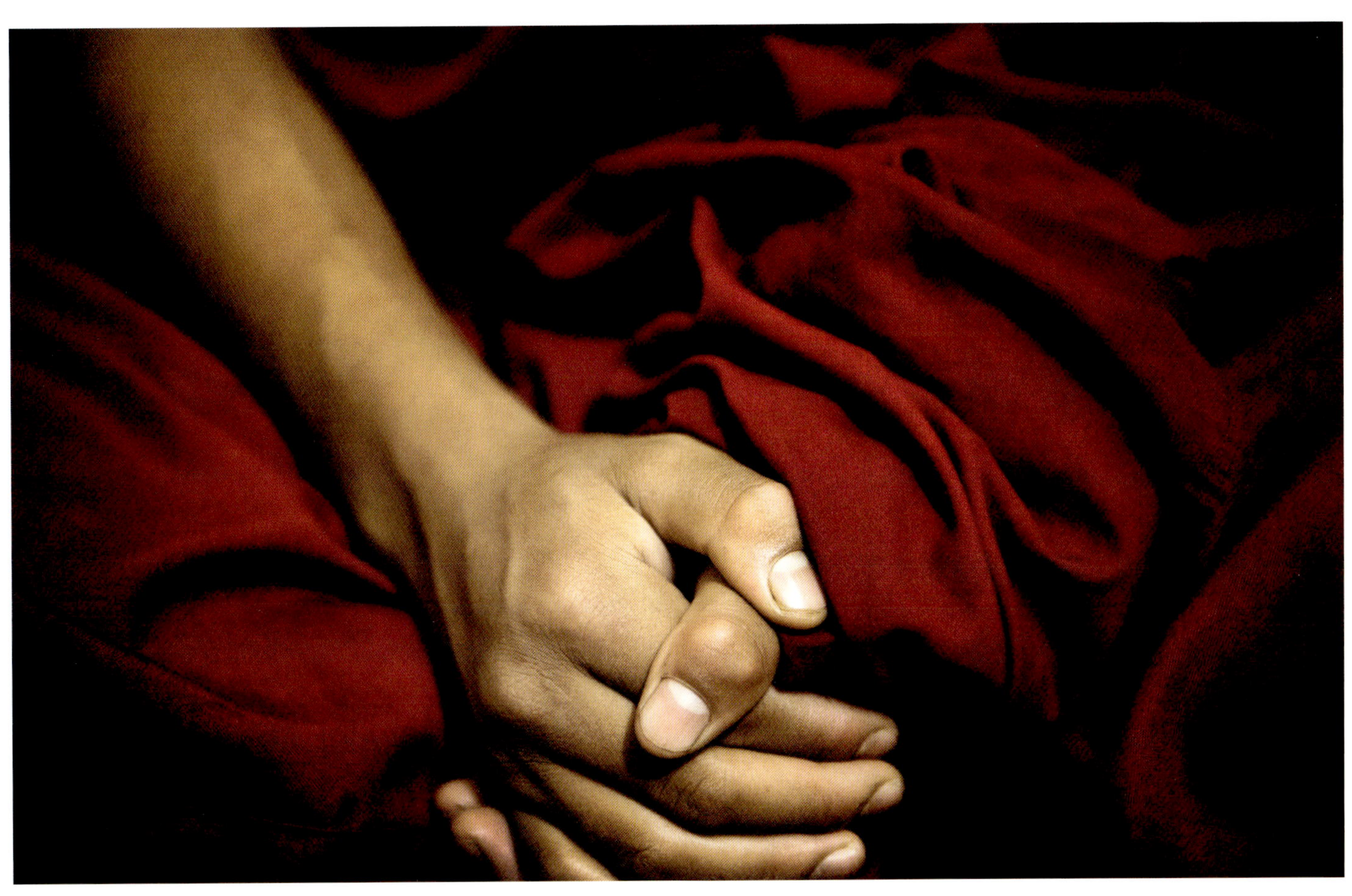

Action without desire.

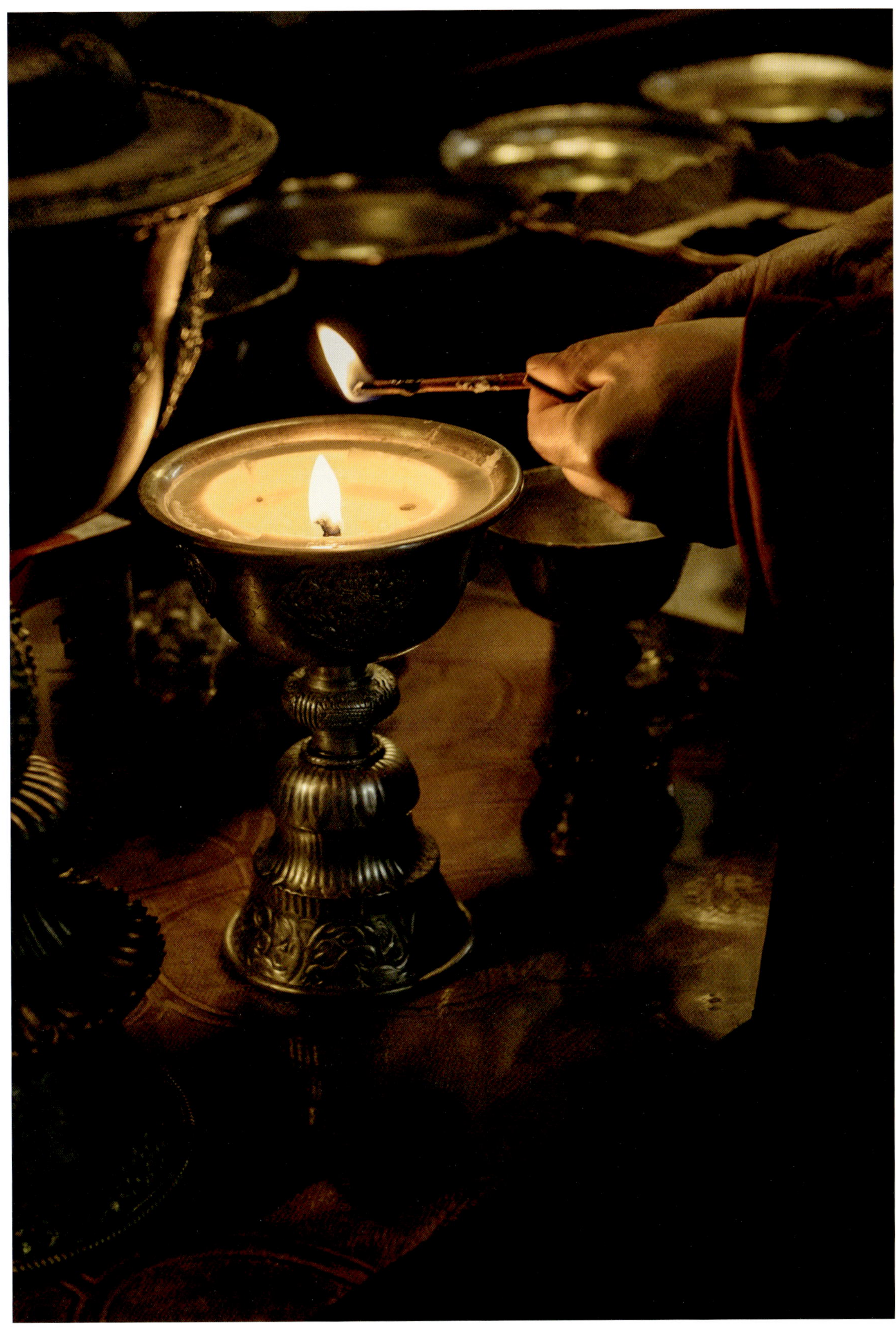

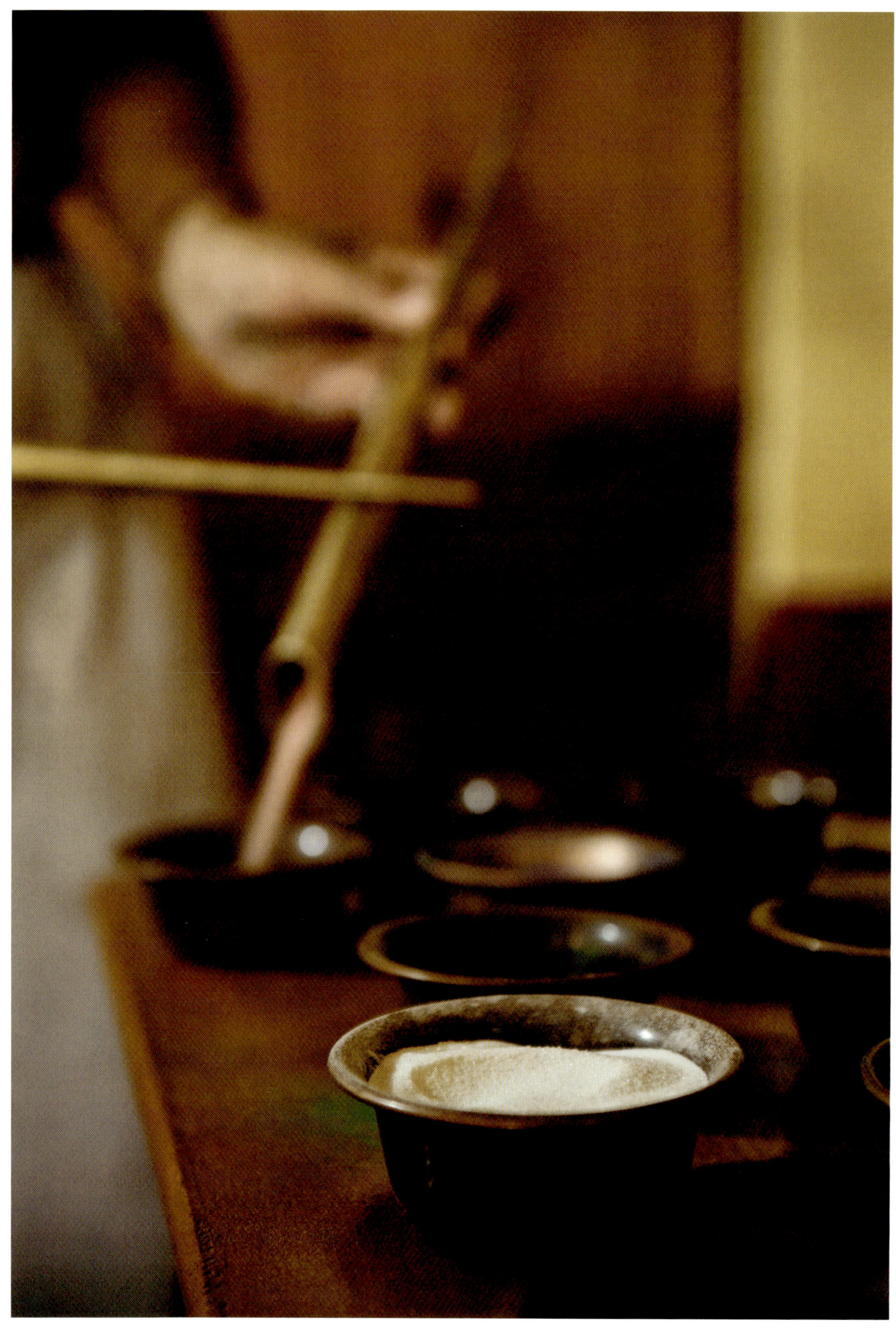

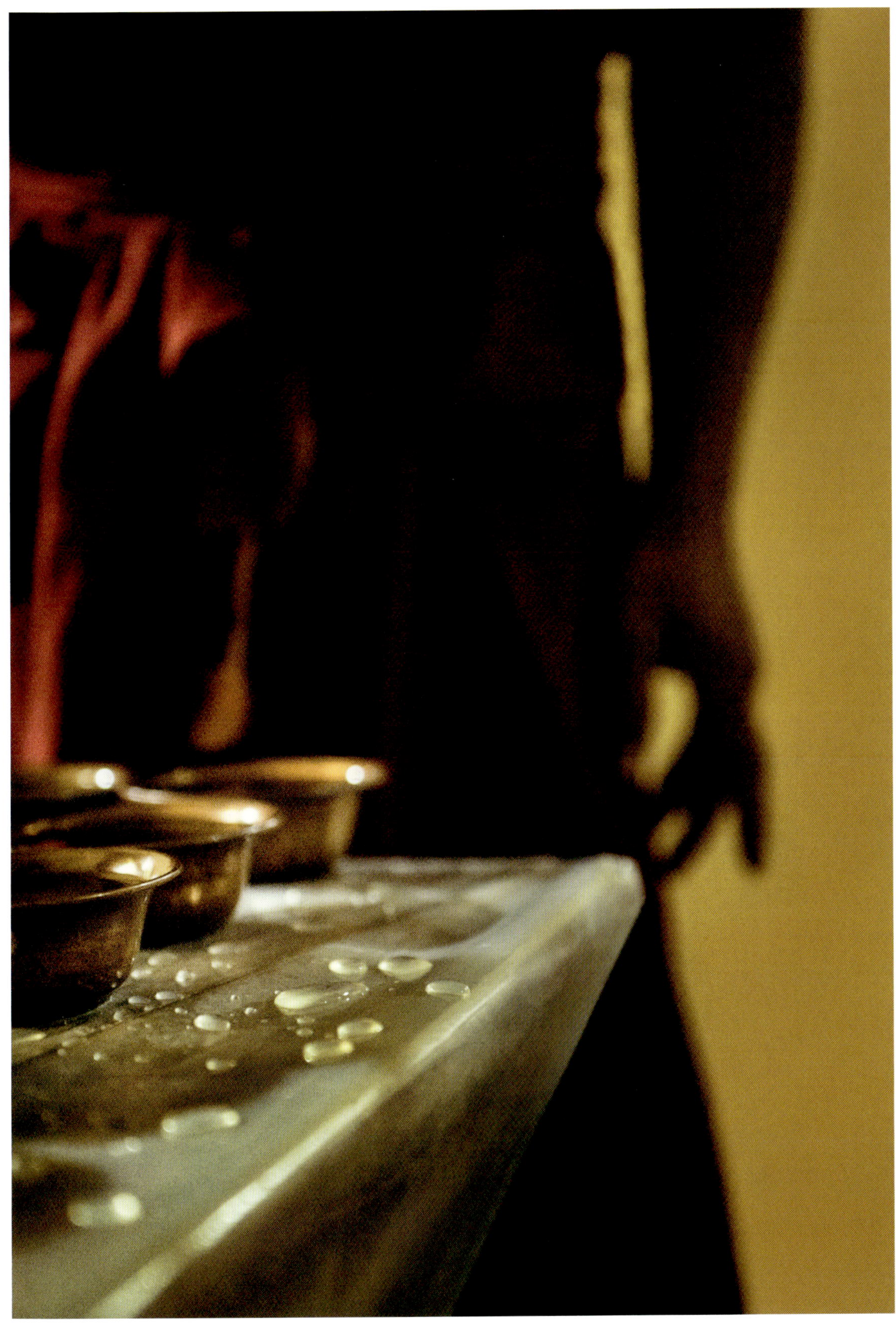

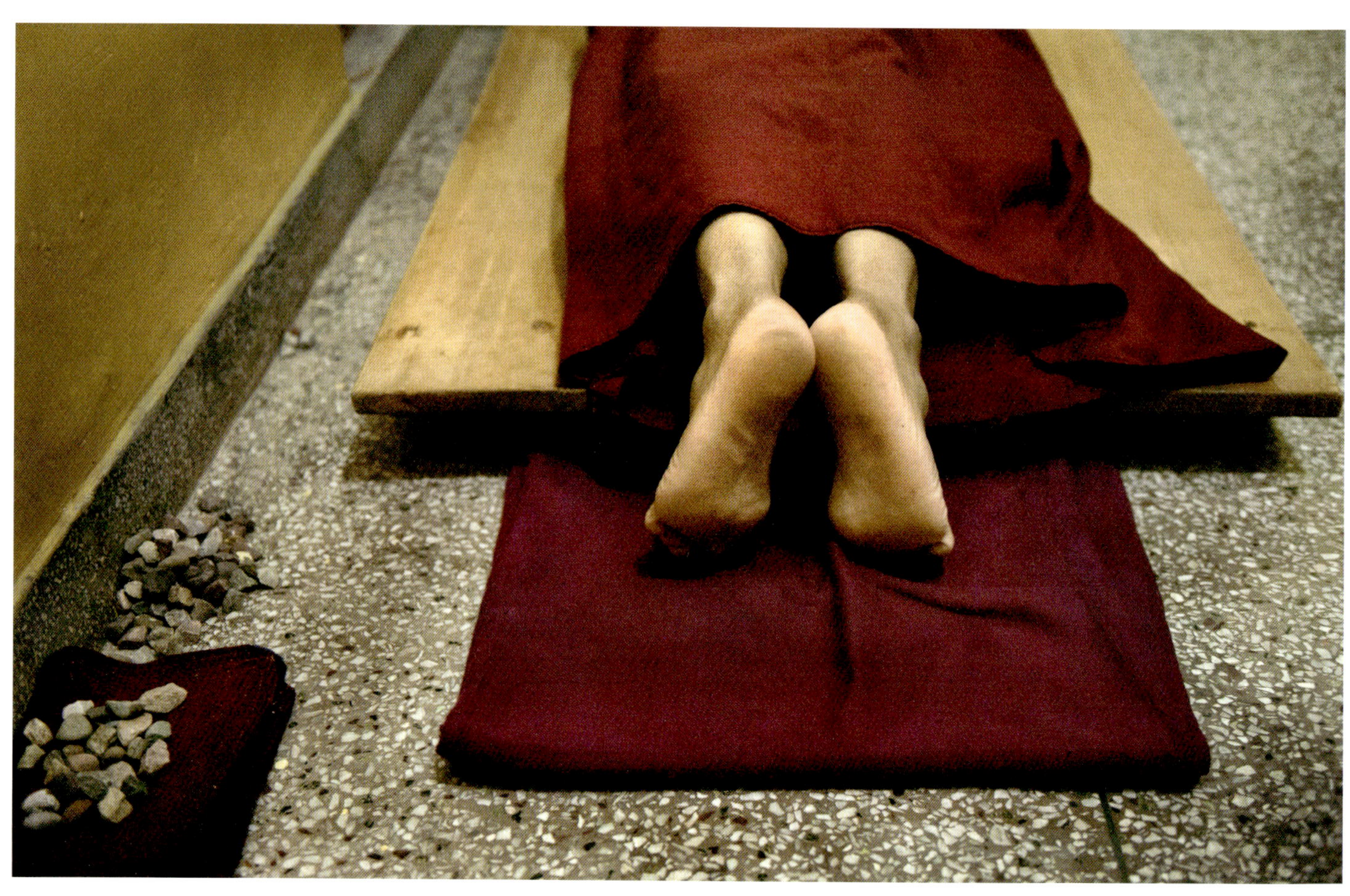

Do not make yourself into anything.

Thoughts rise, let them, they pass.

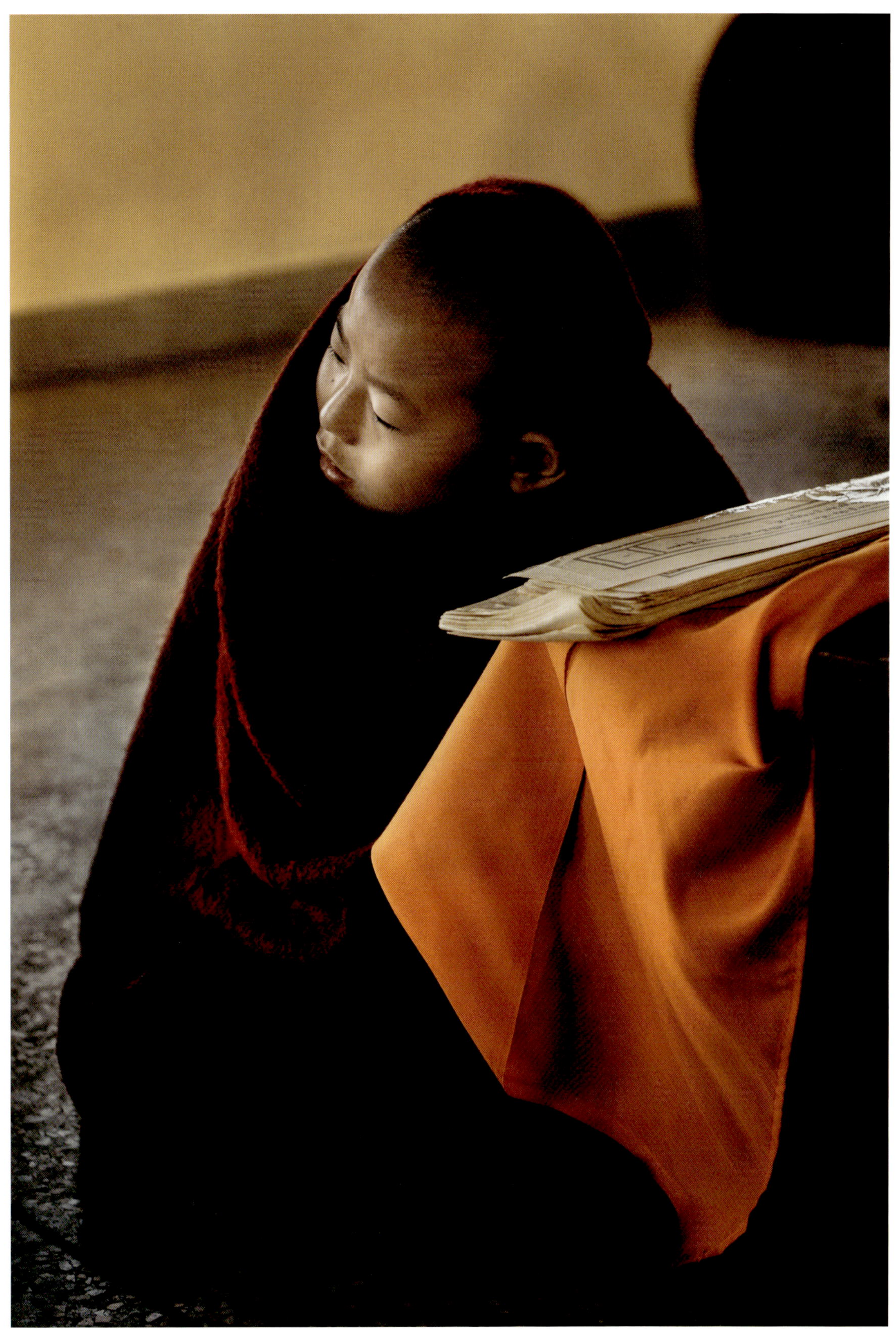

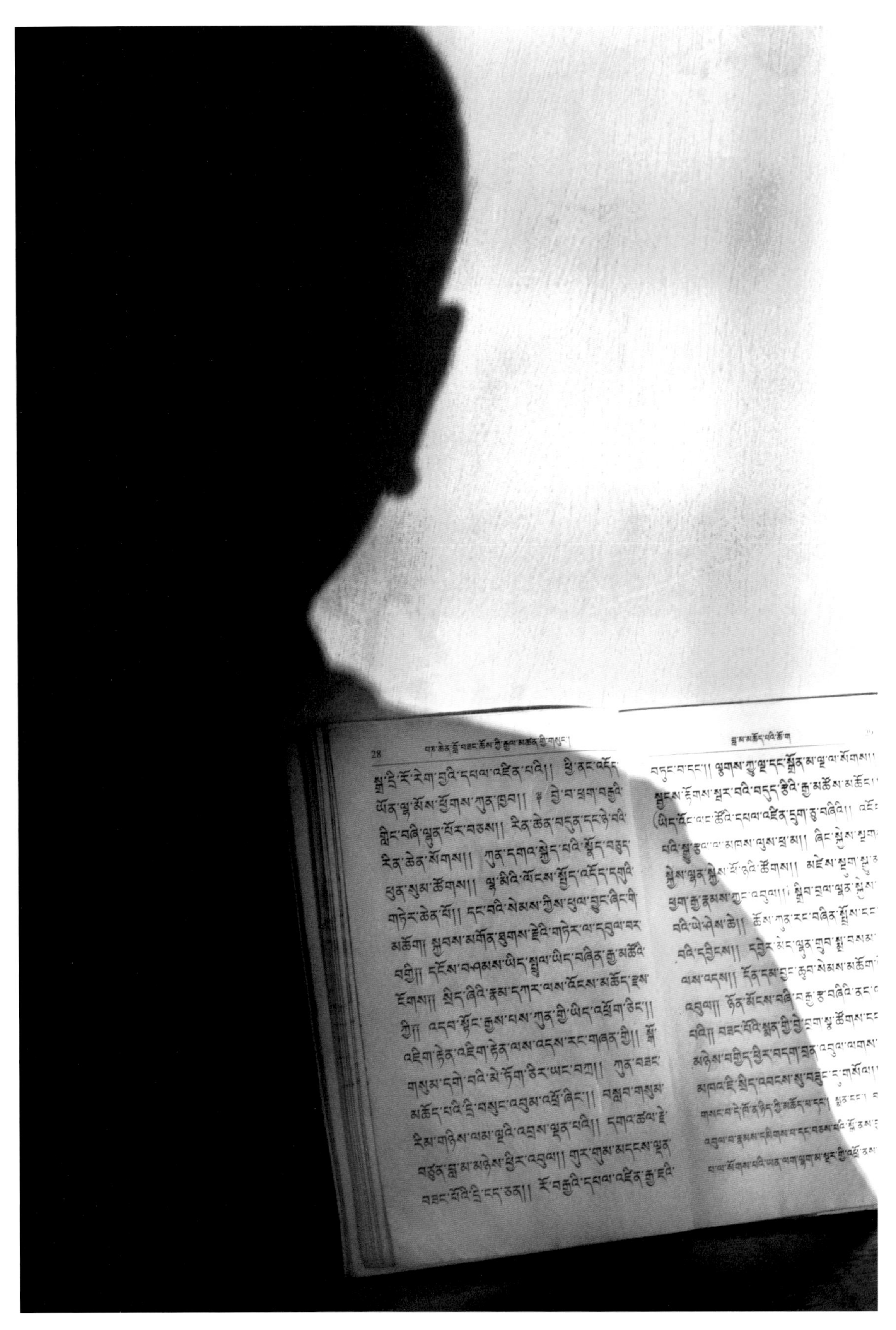

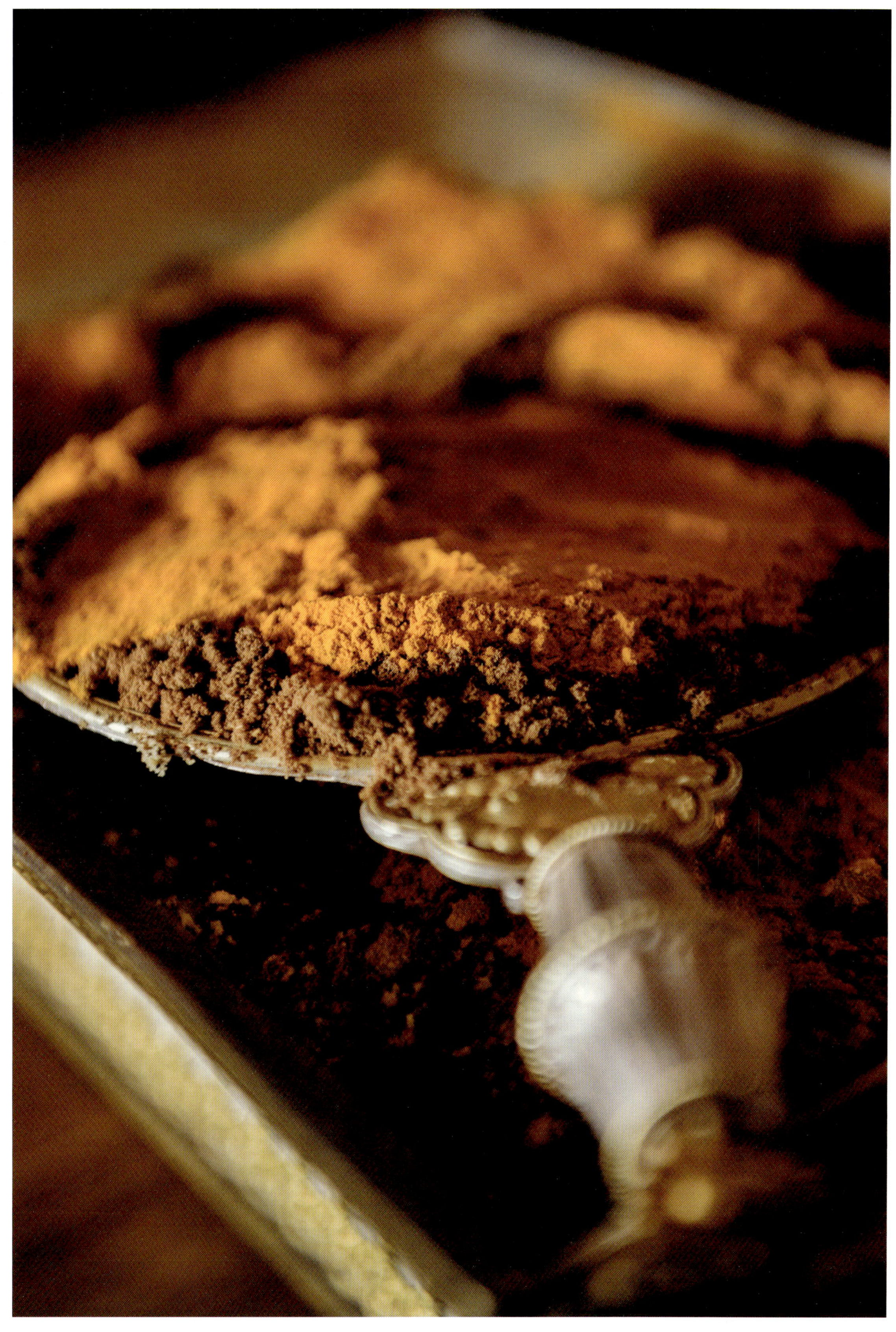

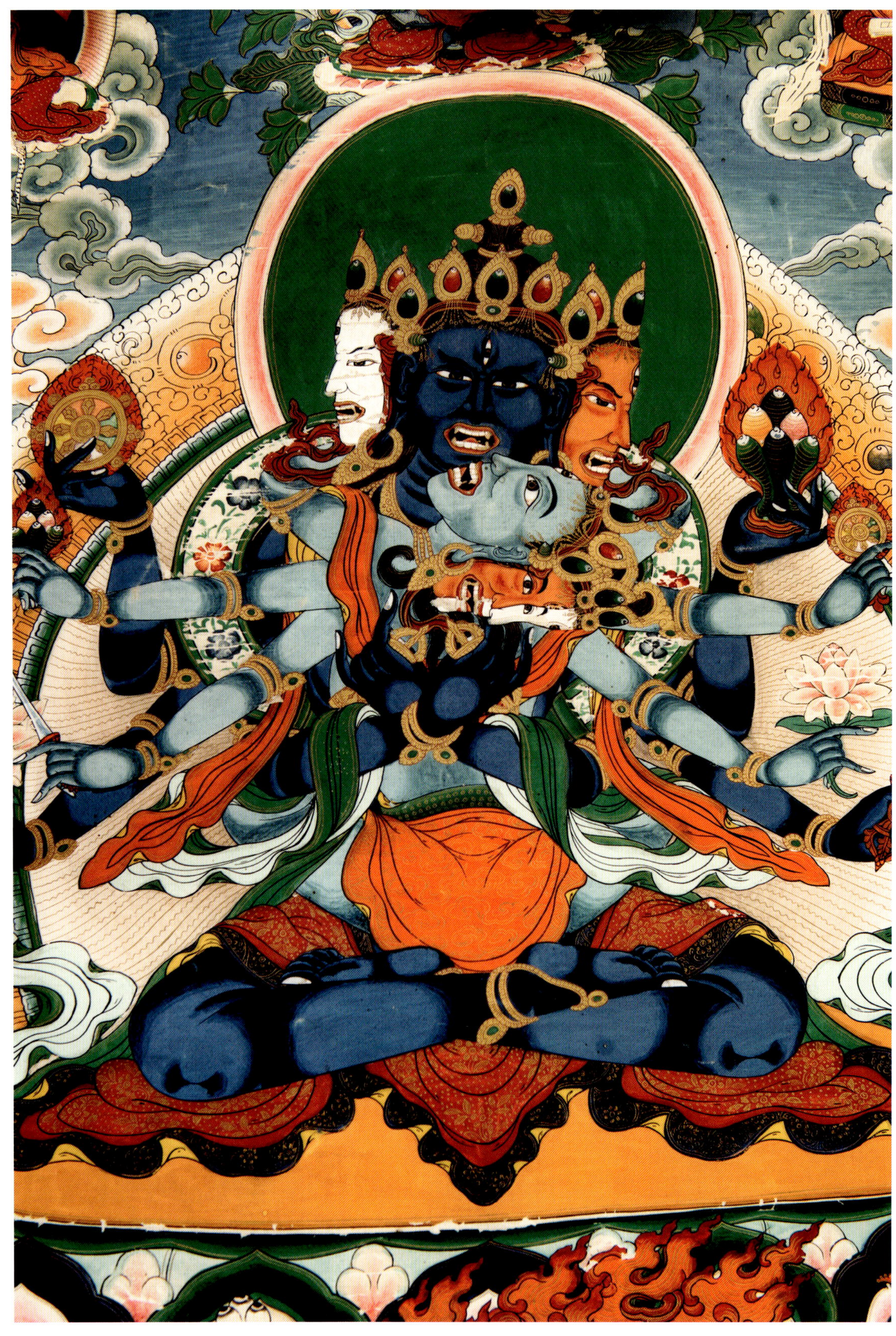

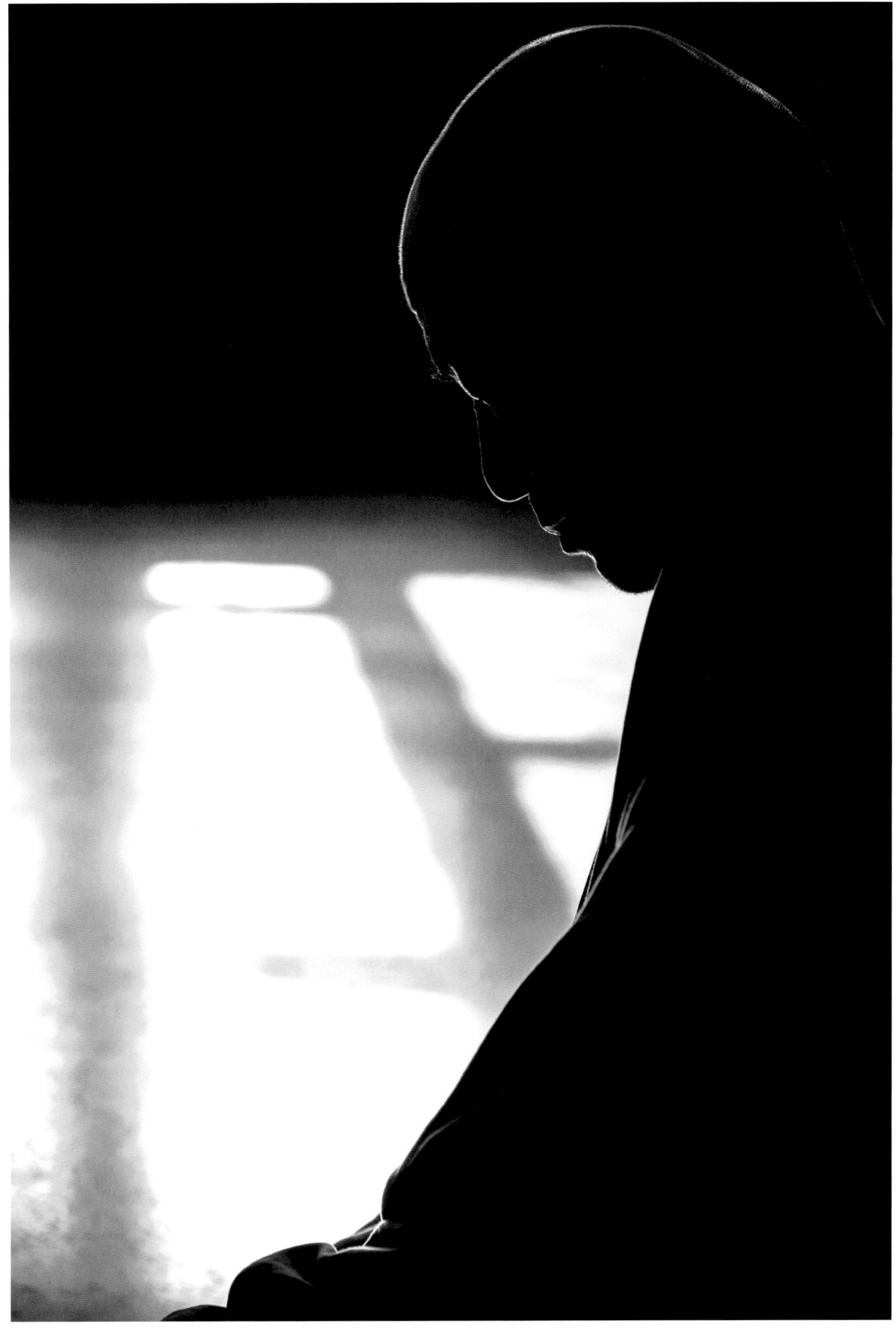

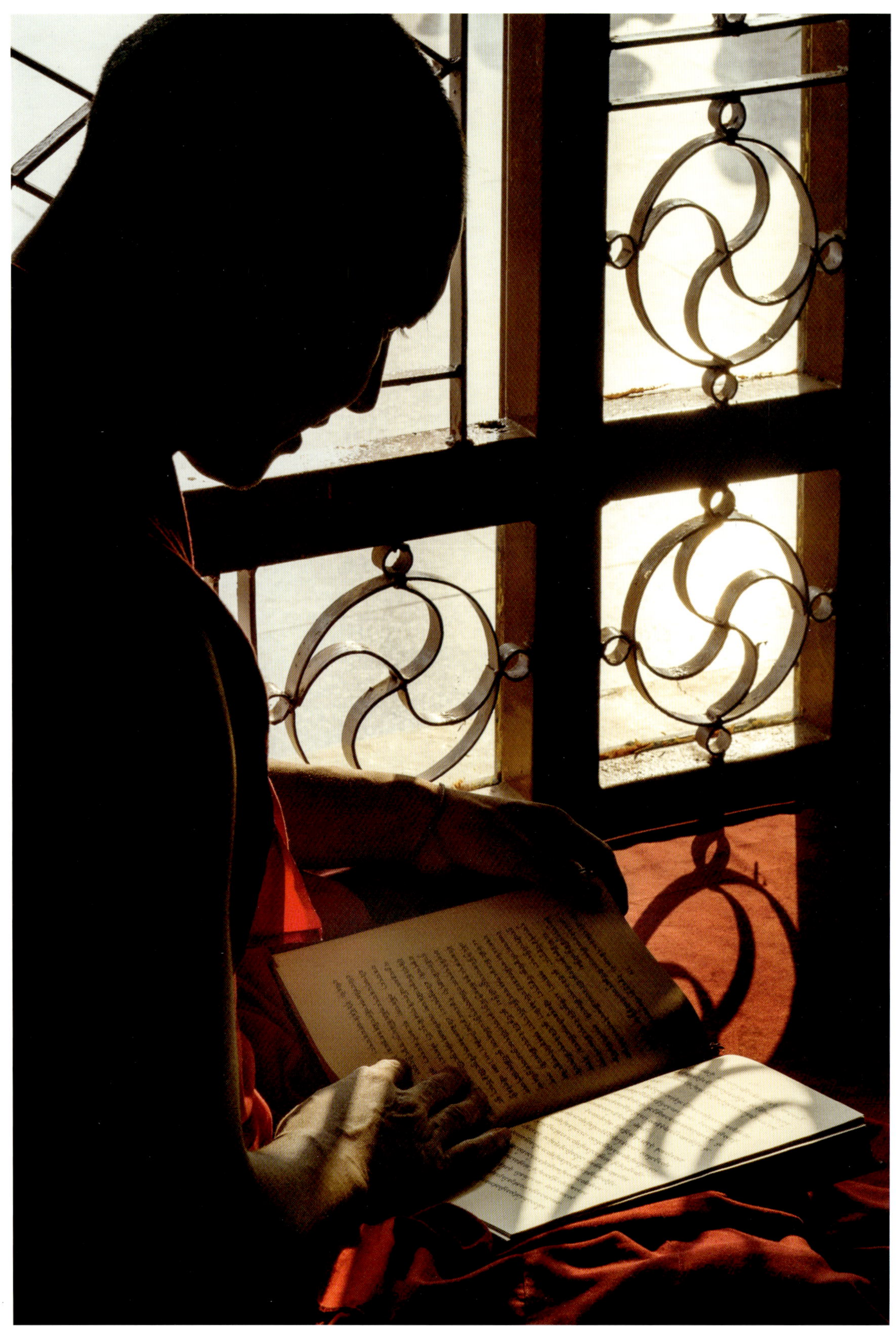

View all problems as challenges.

The Unique Sound Of The Gyuto Monks

Different monasteries have different sounds. Unique to Gyuto Tantric Monastery is a very deep harmonic overtone chanting where each monk produces three octaves at once.

Needing to deeply meditate to produce this sound, their chanting is believed to have a transformative effect on the listener and produces a healing energy for the environment.

These chants are secret and sacred. So sacred in fact that the words are deliberately slurred and made unrecognisable, even to Tibetans.

The chanting is hard to learn. It is taught from a young age and takes lots of practice. Some monks are naturals, others struggle.

Chanting is the third and final piece after memorising and debating the texts. It draws down into their being, into their body, this learning and understanding.

The memorising is the rote learning, the debating allows them to intellectually understand the texts while the chanting integrates it, makes it a part of their actual physical being so that they are living, walking embodiments of the Buddha's teachings.

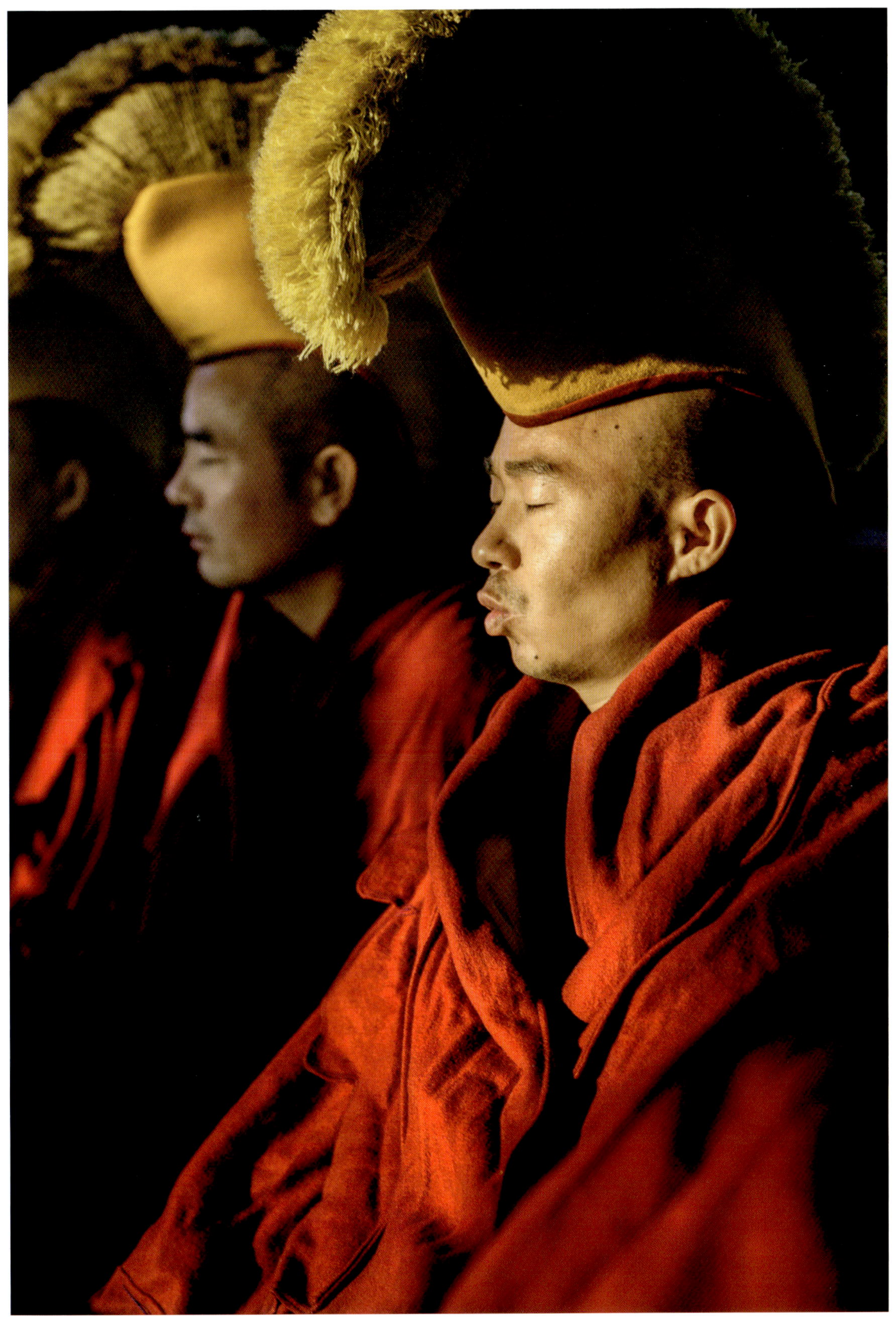

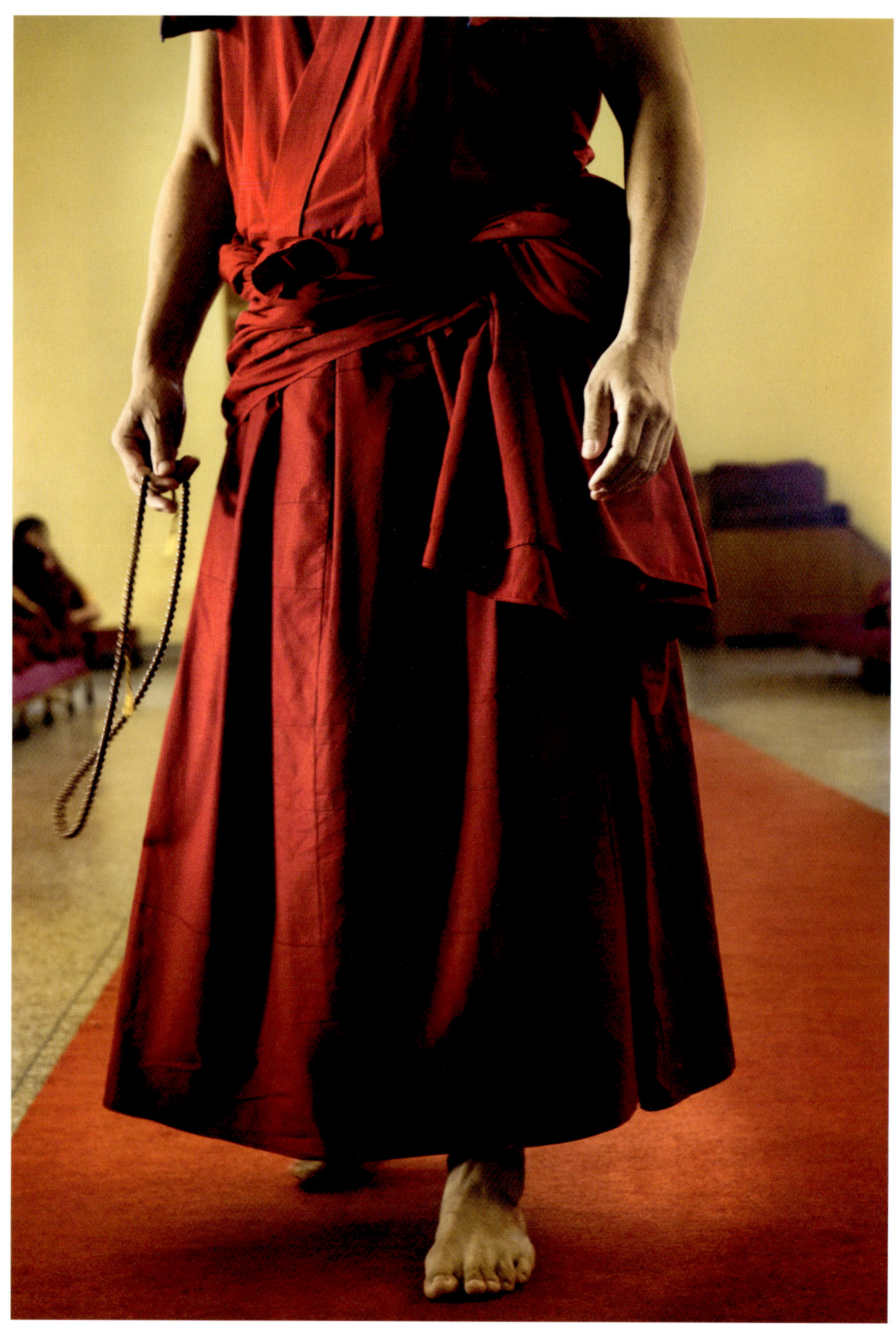

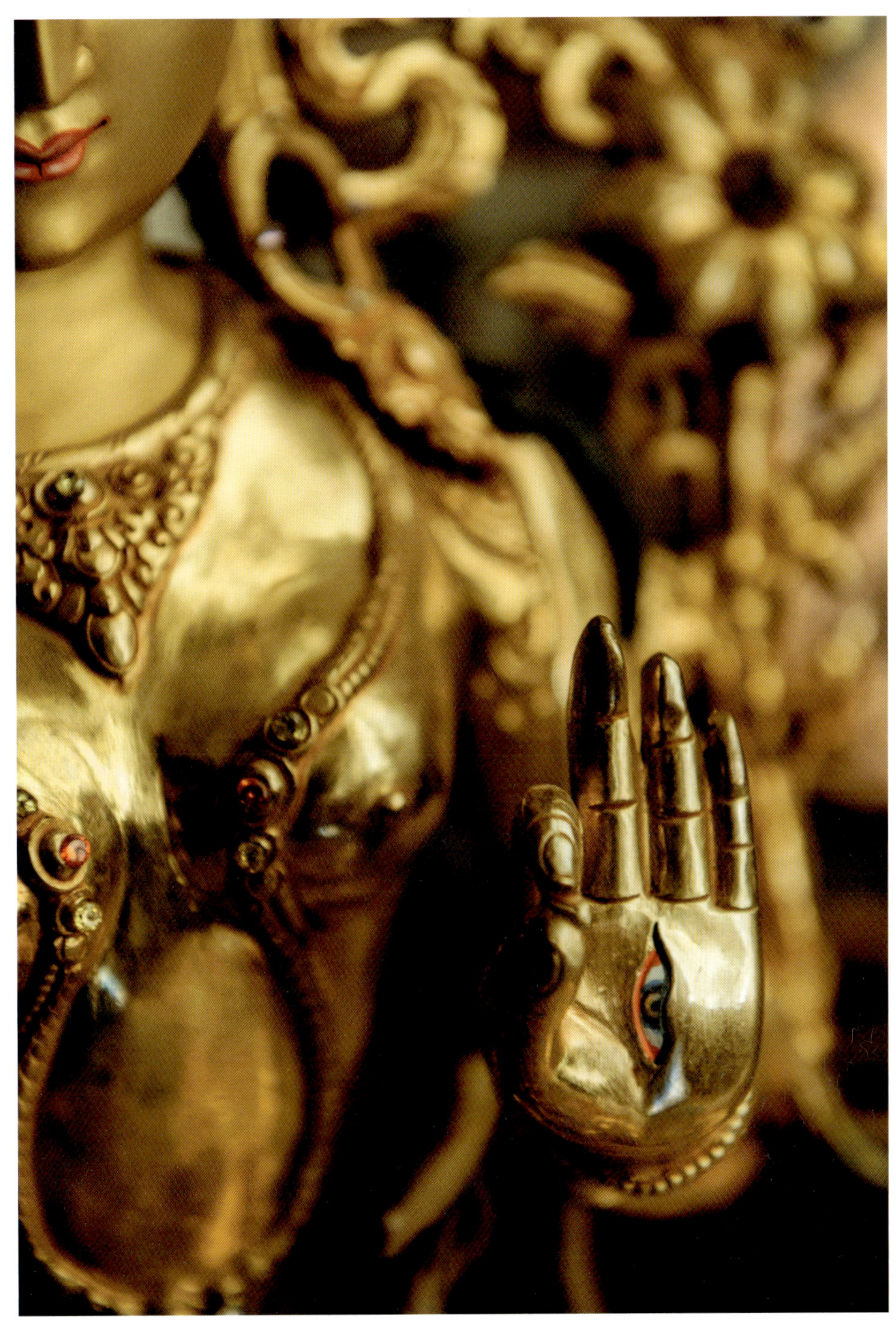

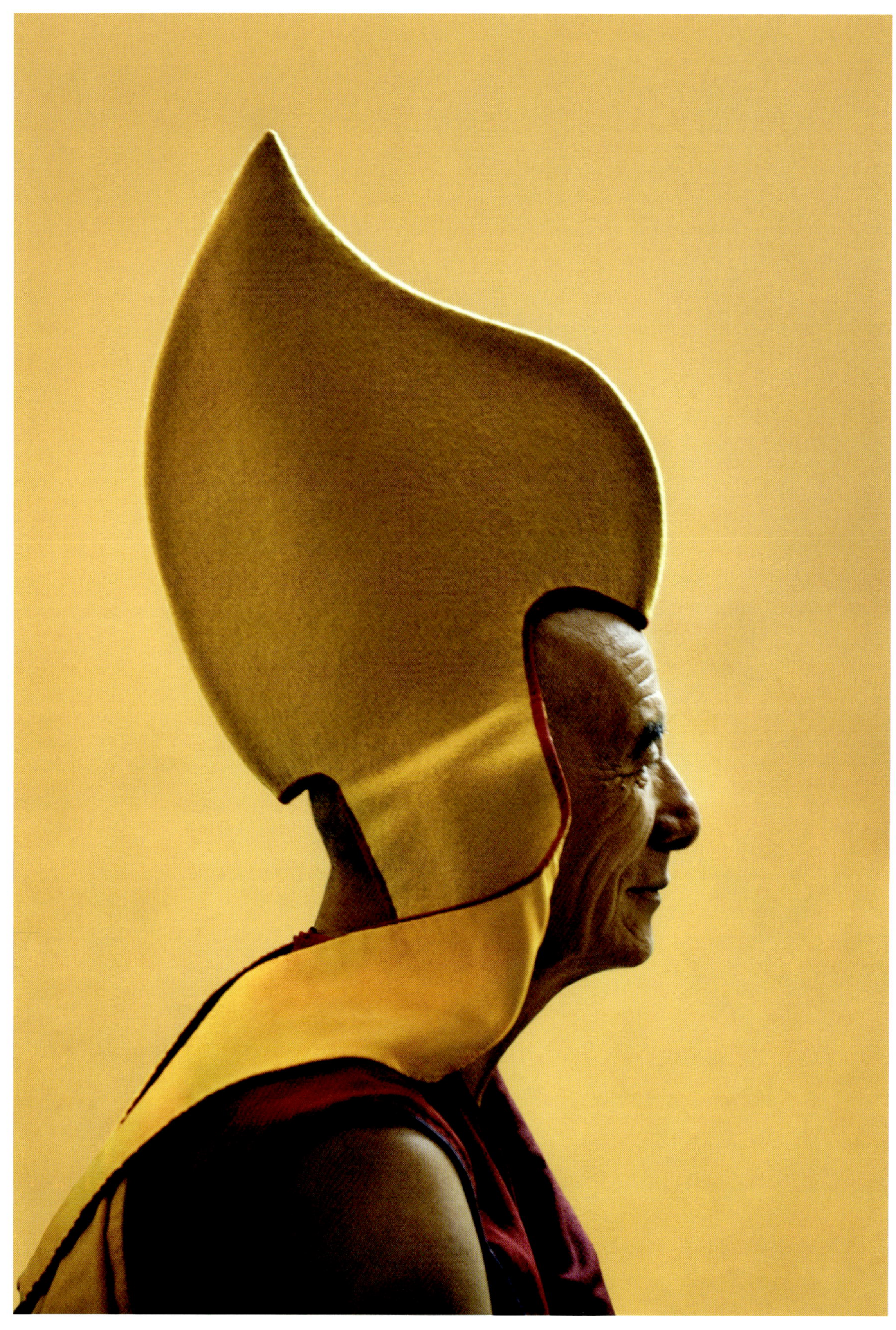

Nature of mind is pure.

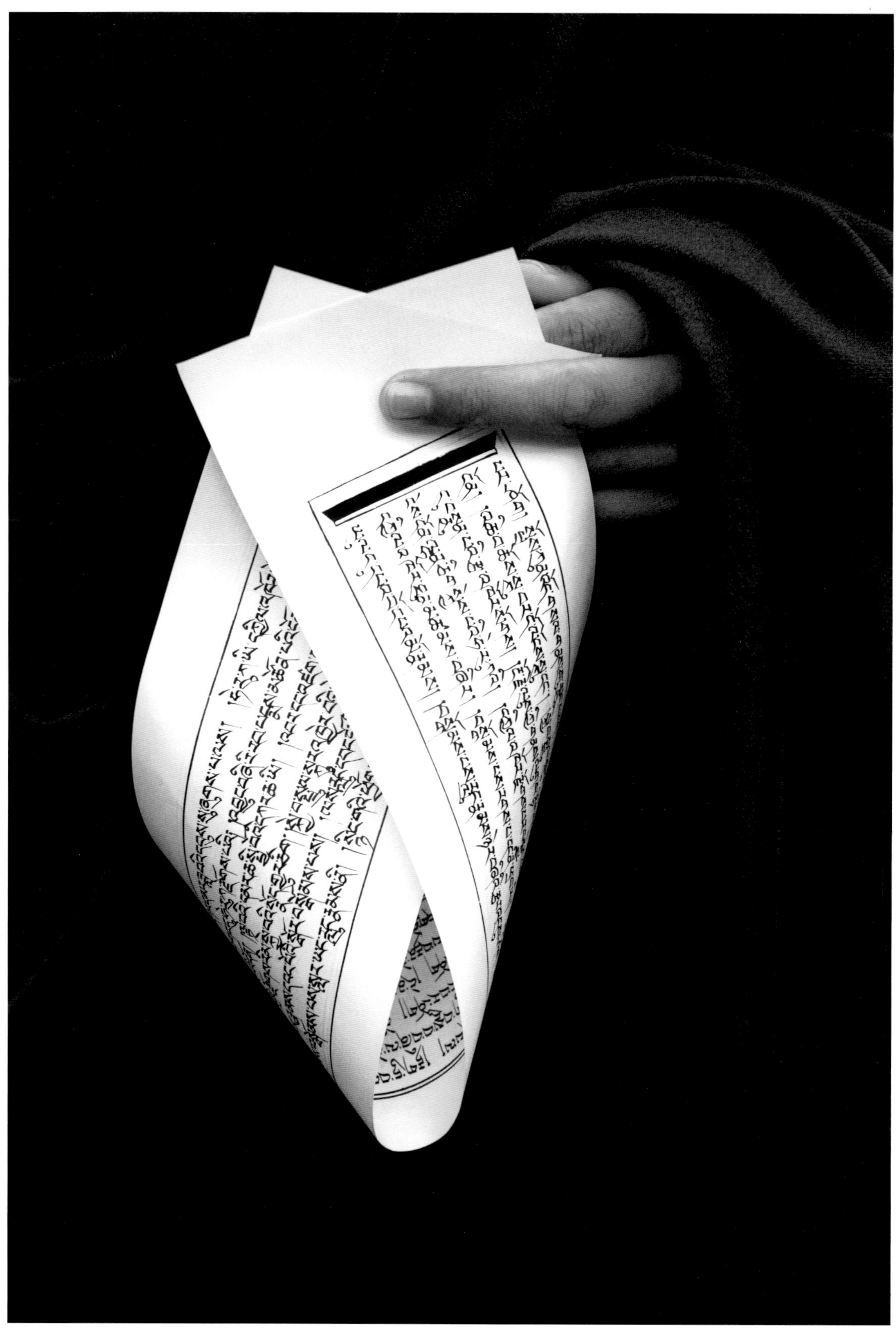

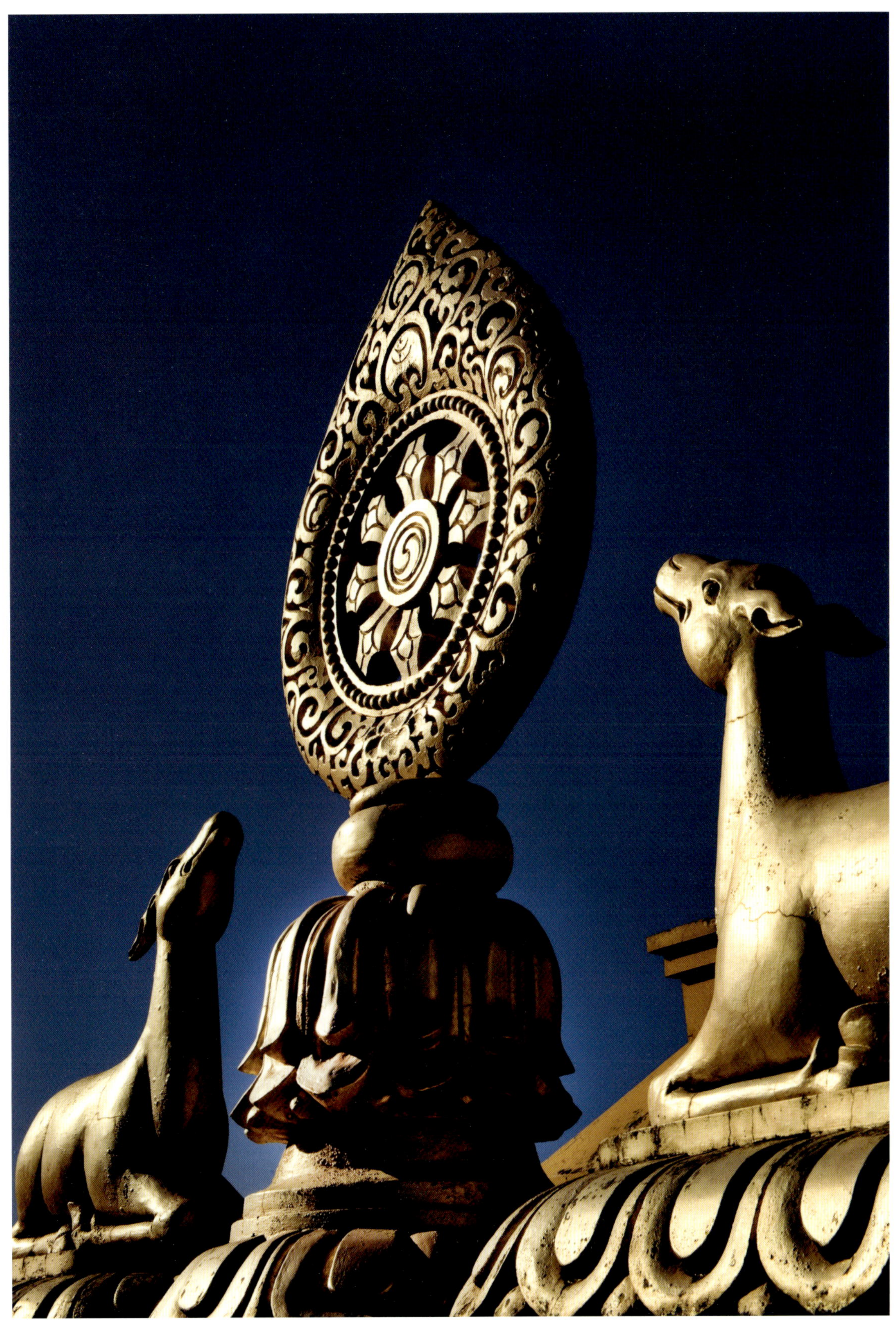

Time passes unhindered.

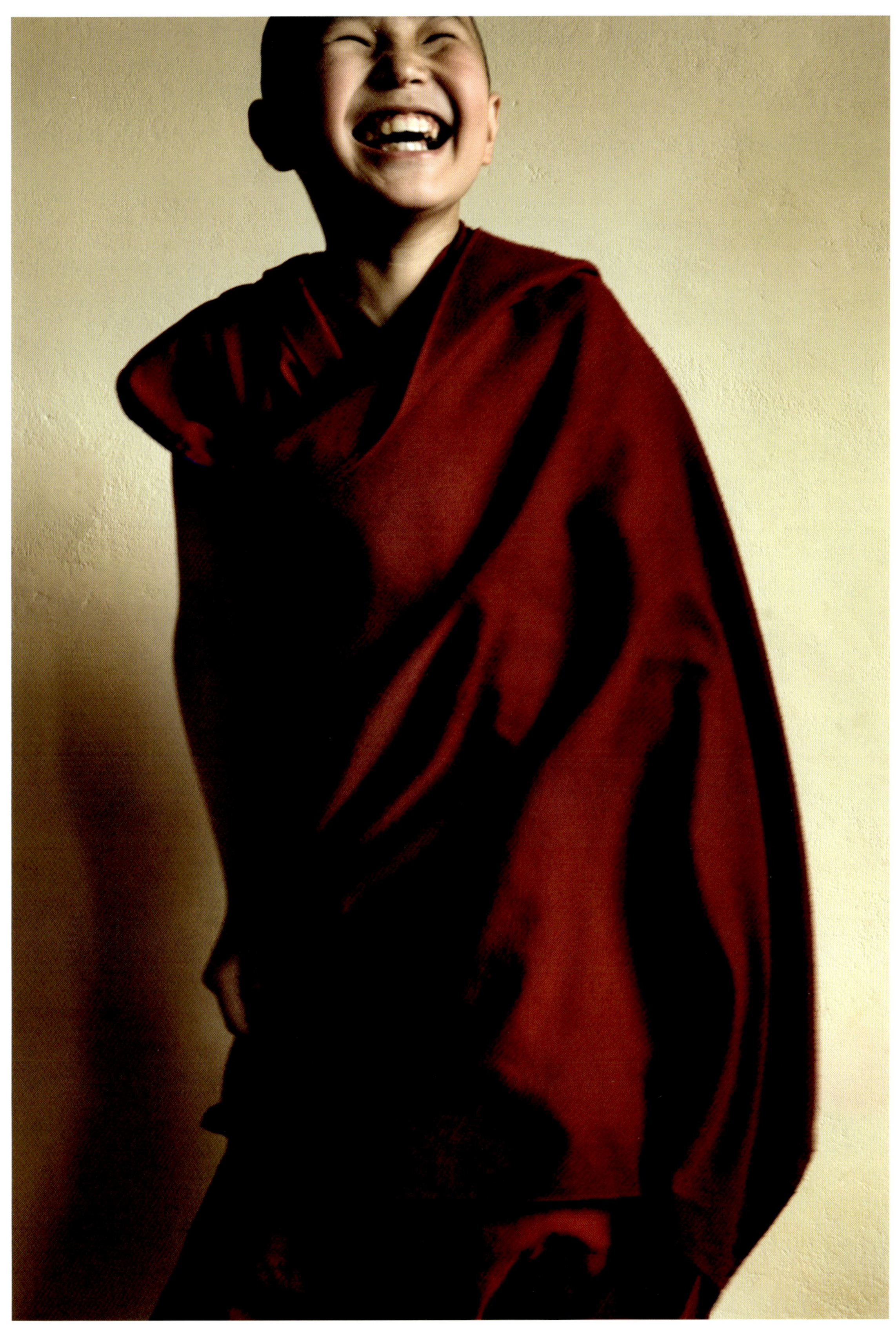

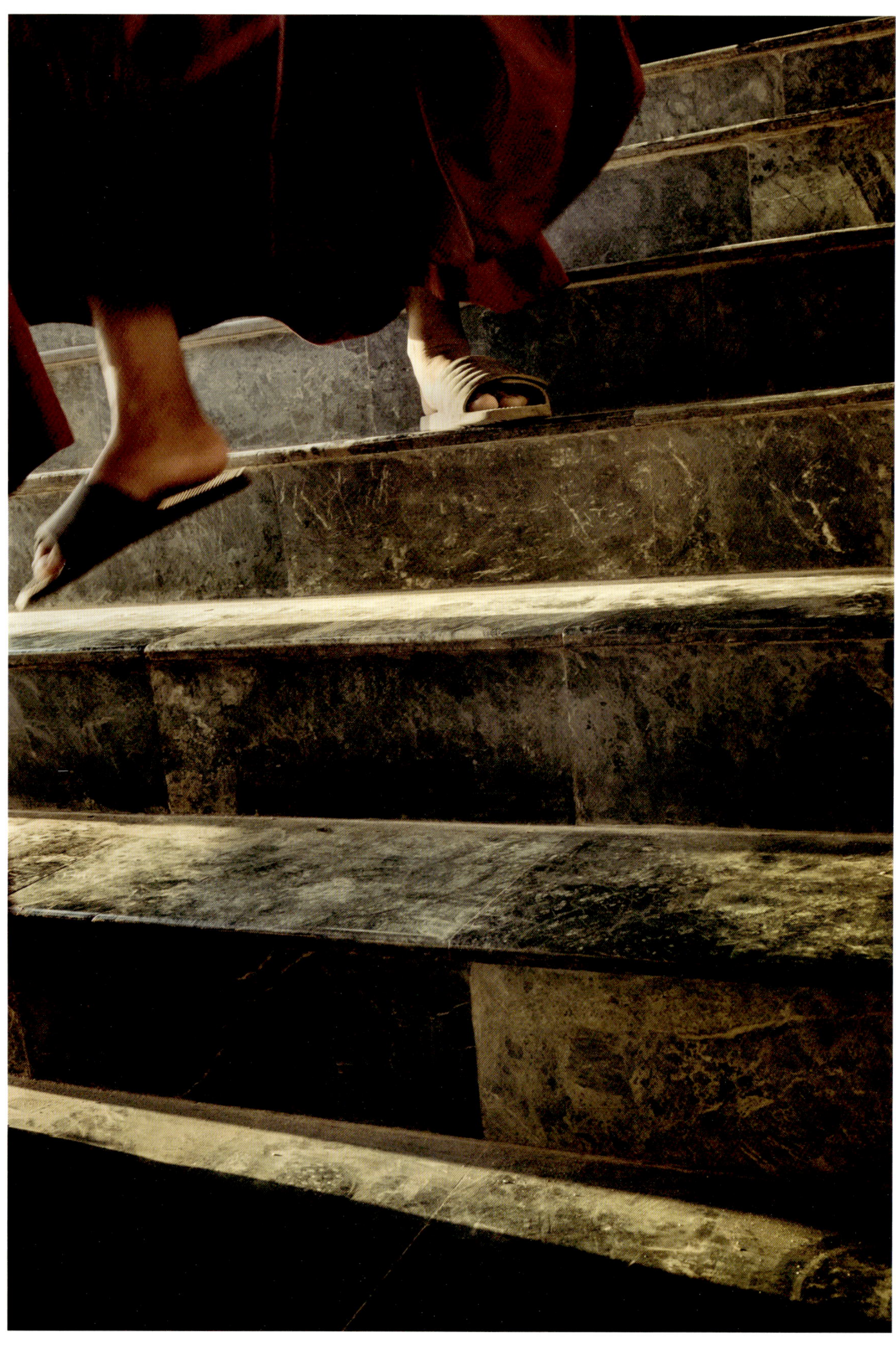

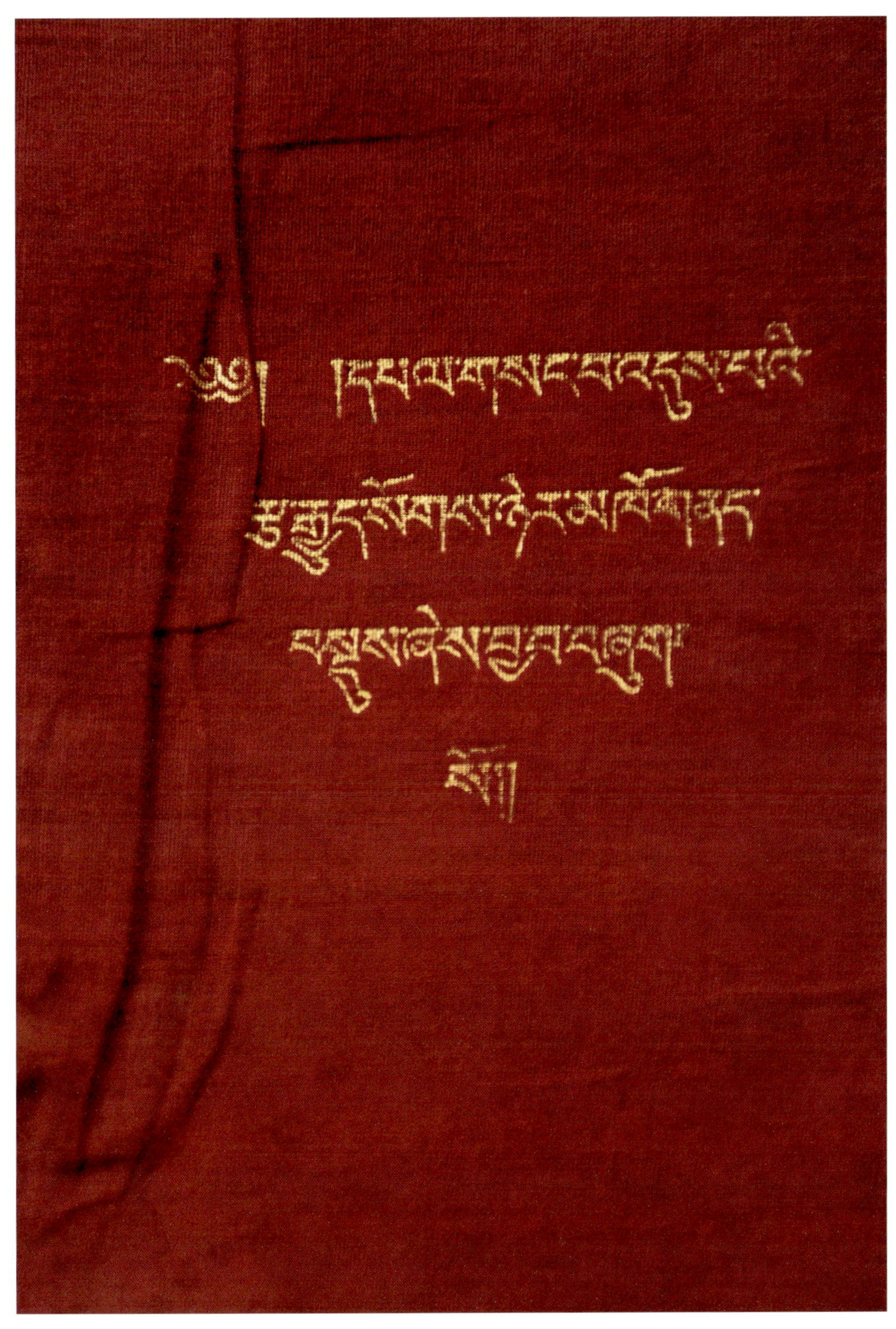
ༀ། །དཔལ་གར་དབང་བདུད་རྩི་པའི
ཅ་རྒྱུད་གསལ་བའི་རིམ་ཡོ་གས་ན
བསྲས་ནས་གྲུབ་པ་ལུགས།
རྫོག

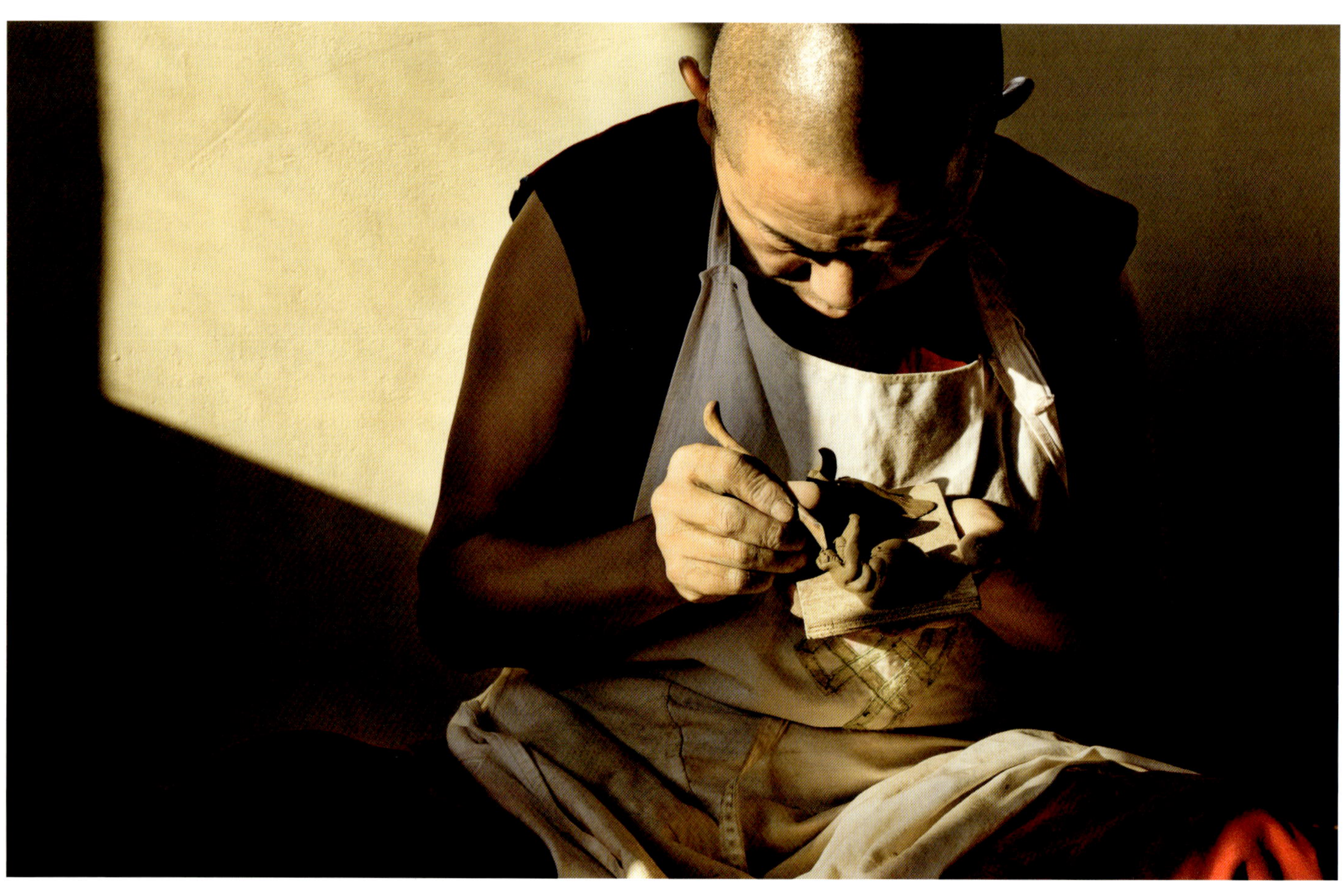

Delusion is a product of belief.

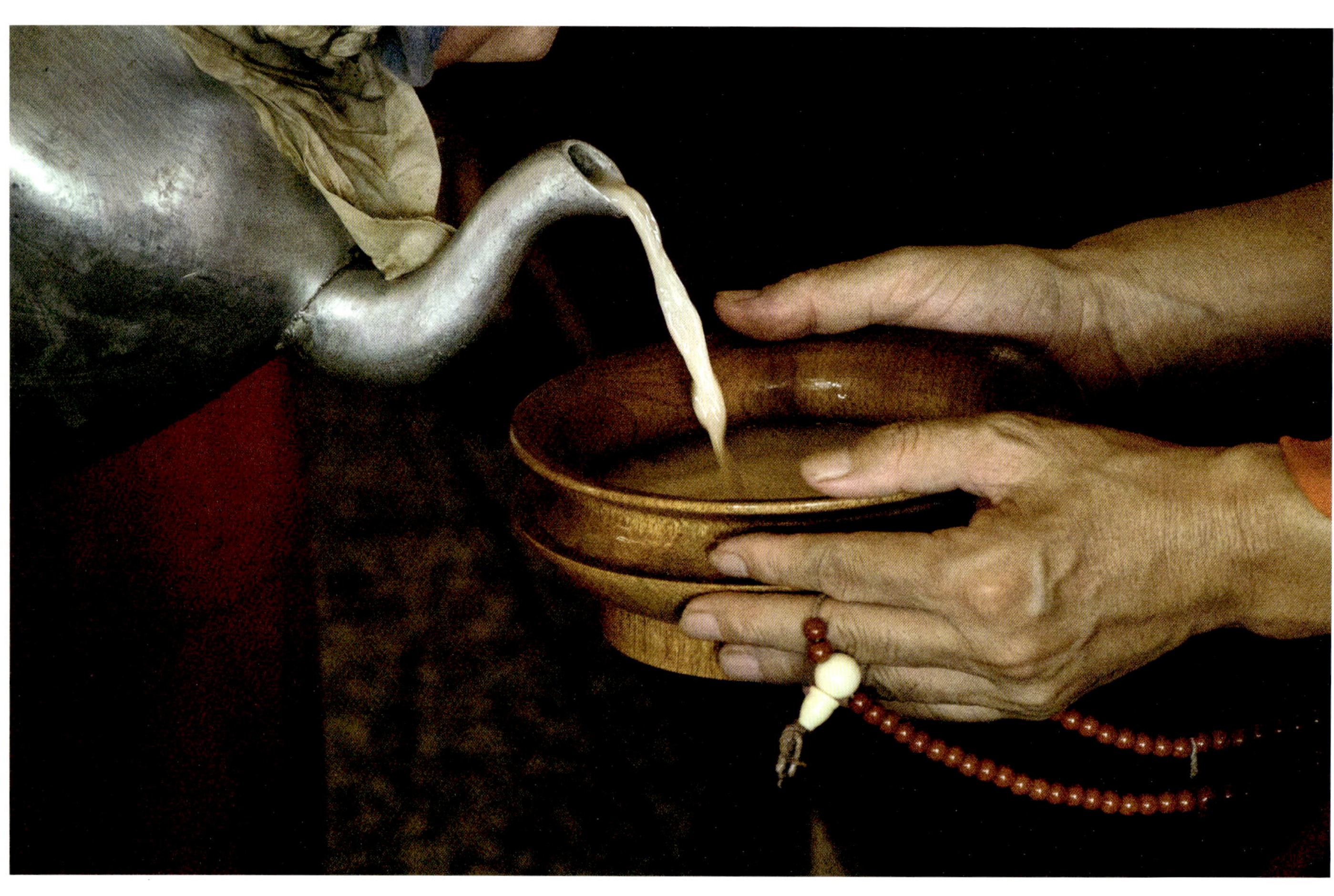

It's always possible to be kind.

Reaction is a choice.

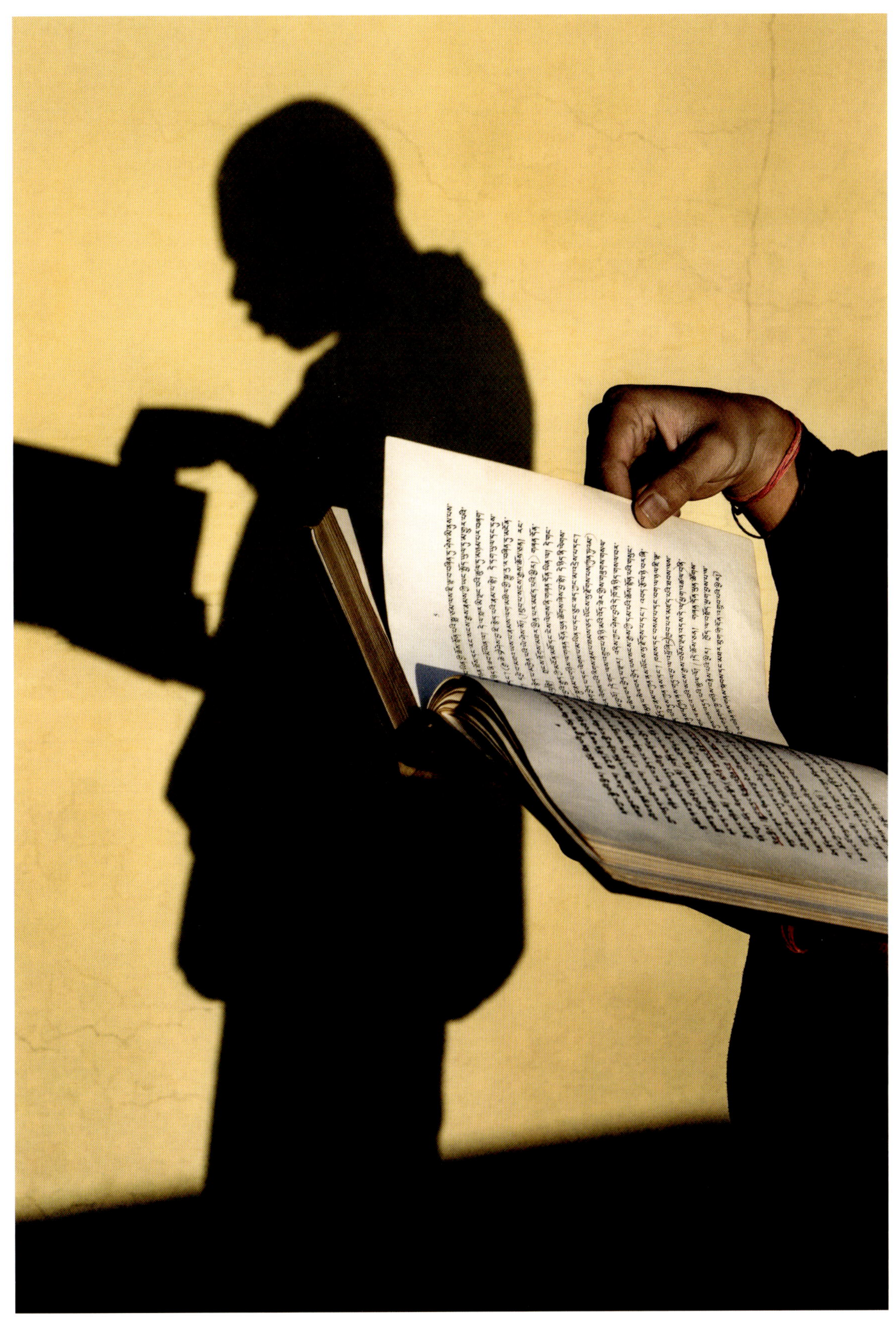

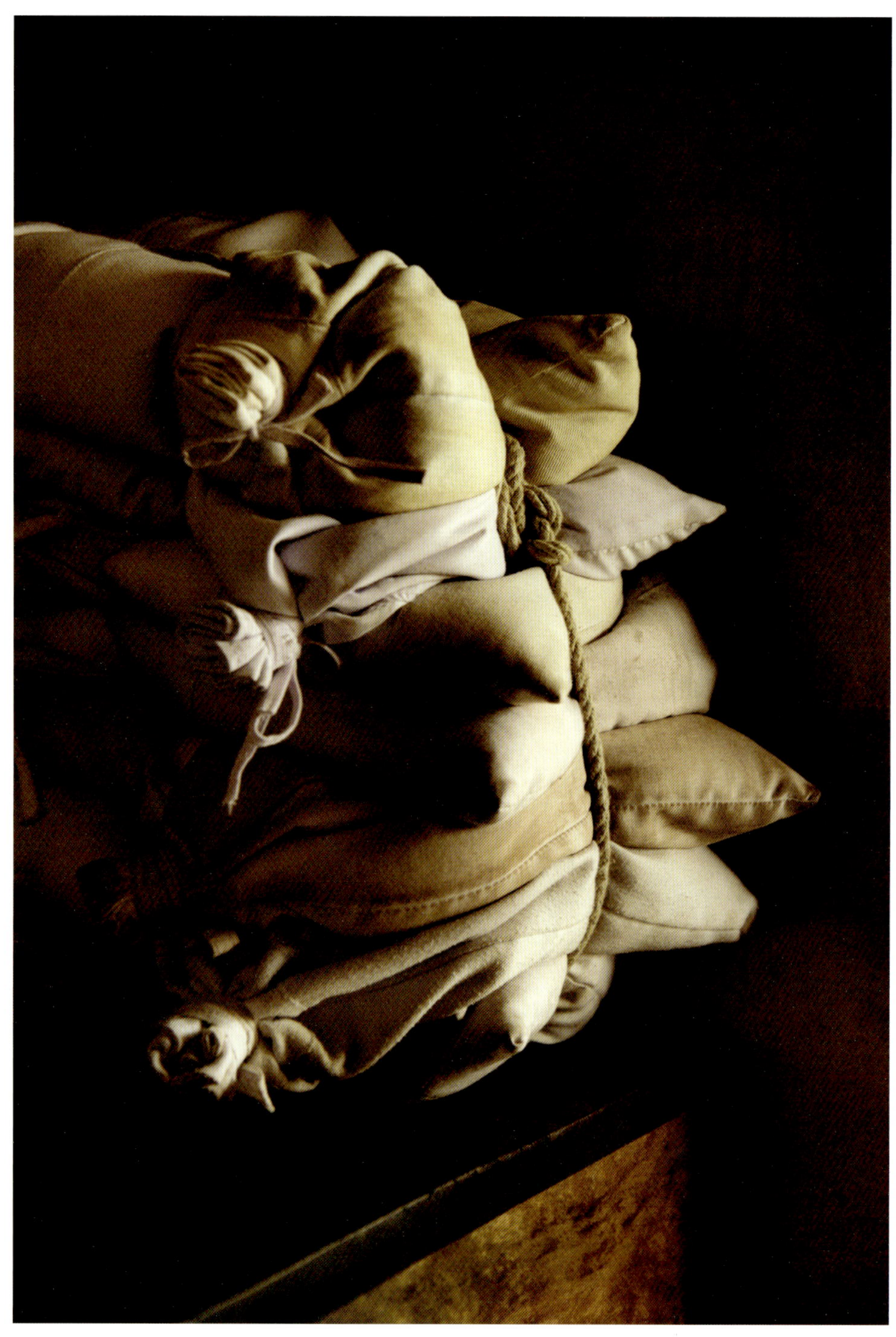

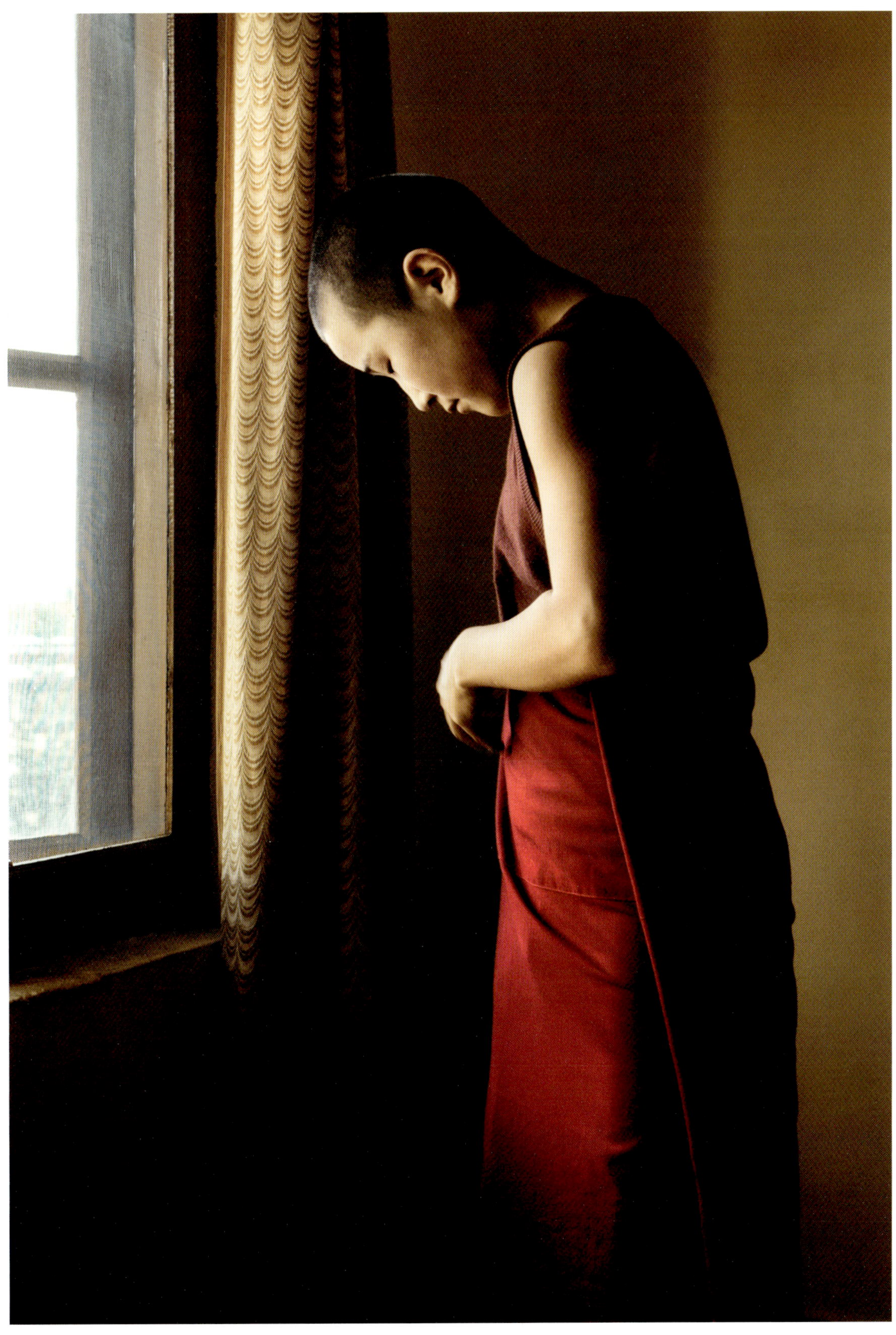

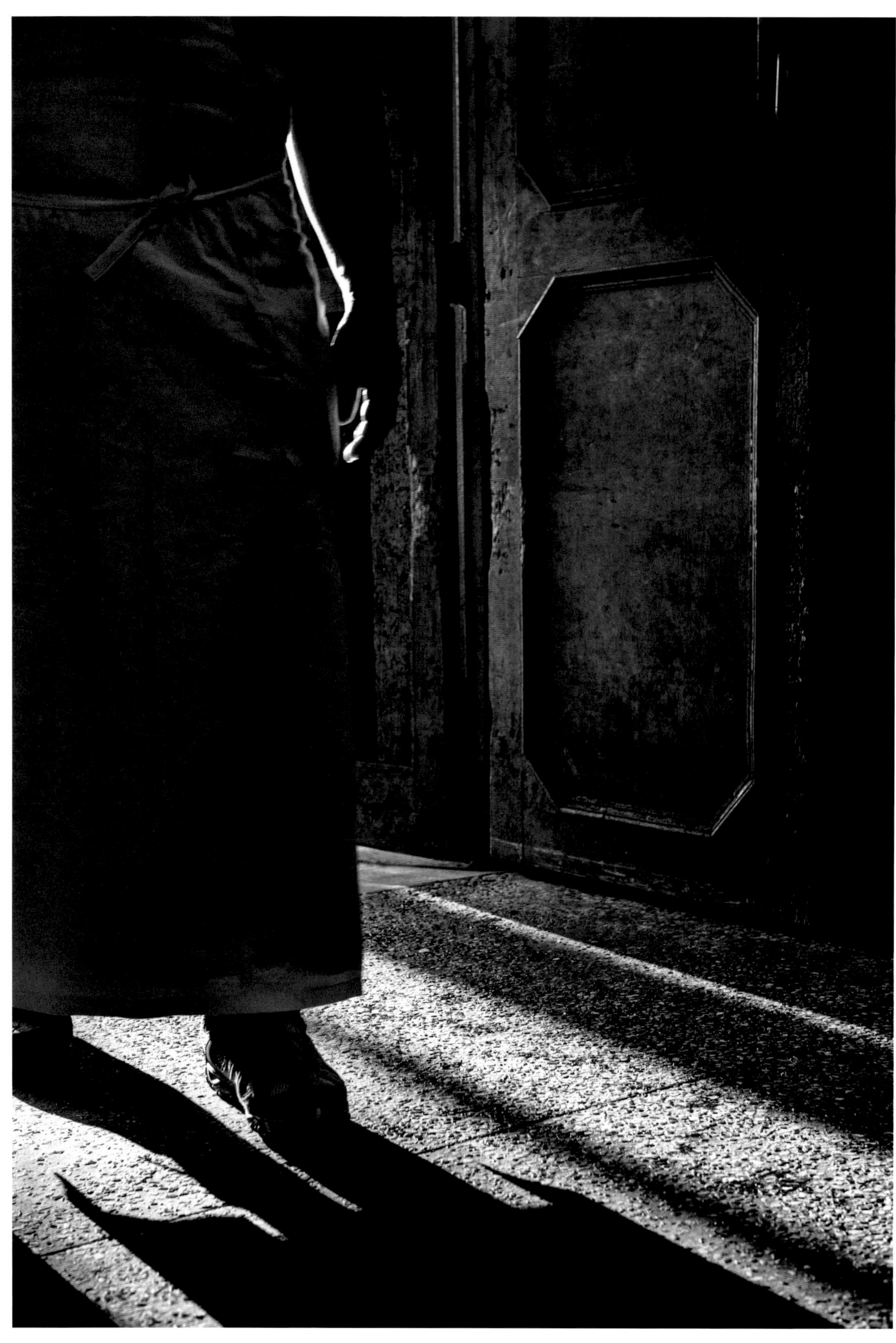

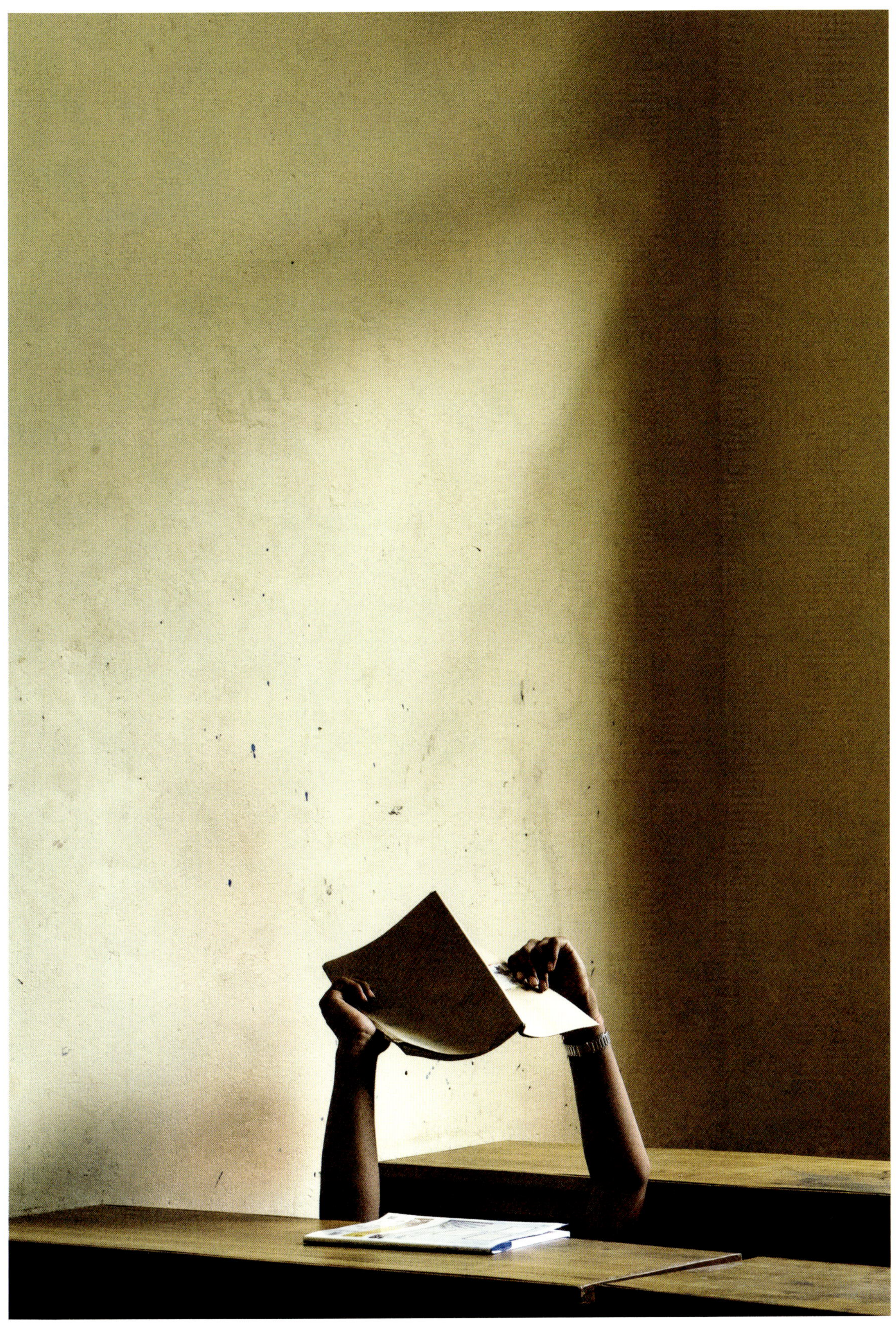

Gratitude.

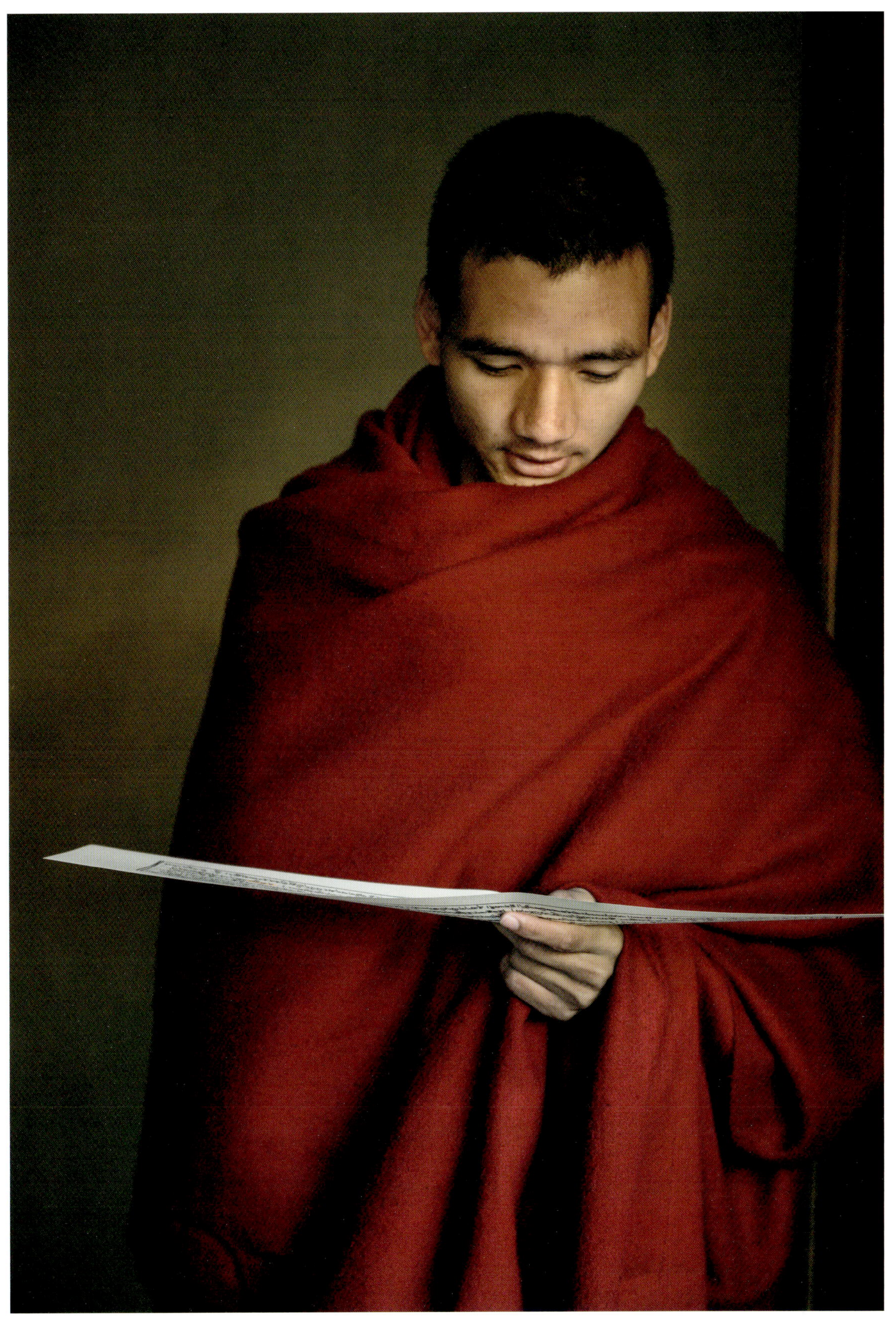

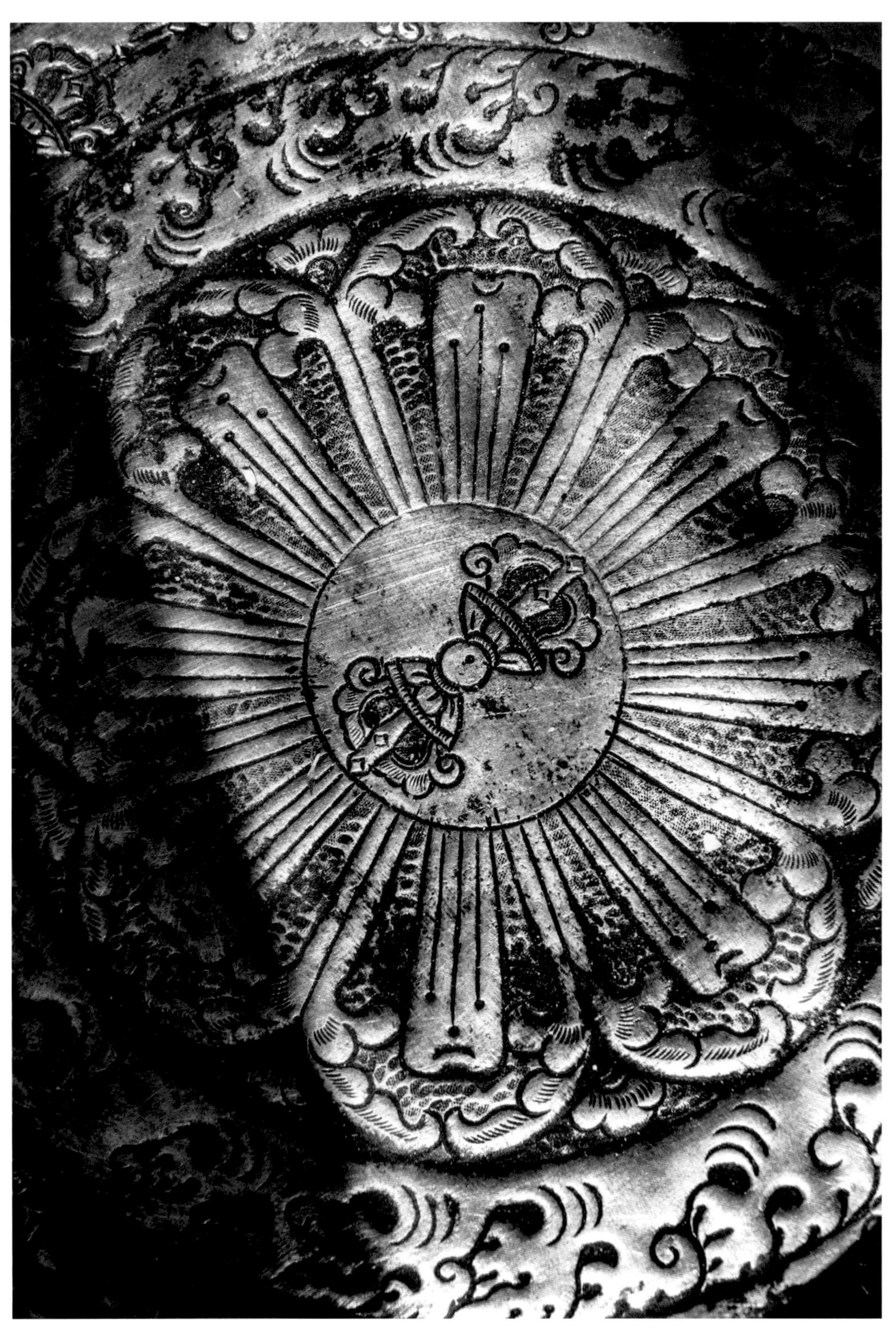

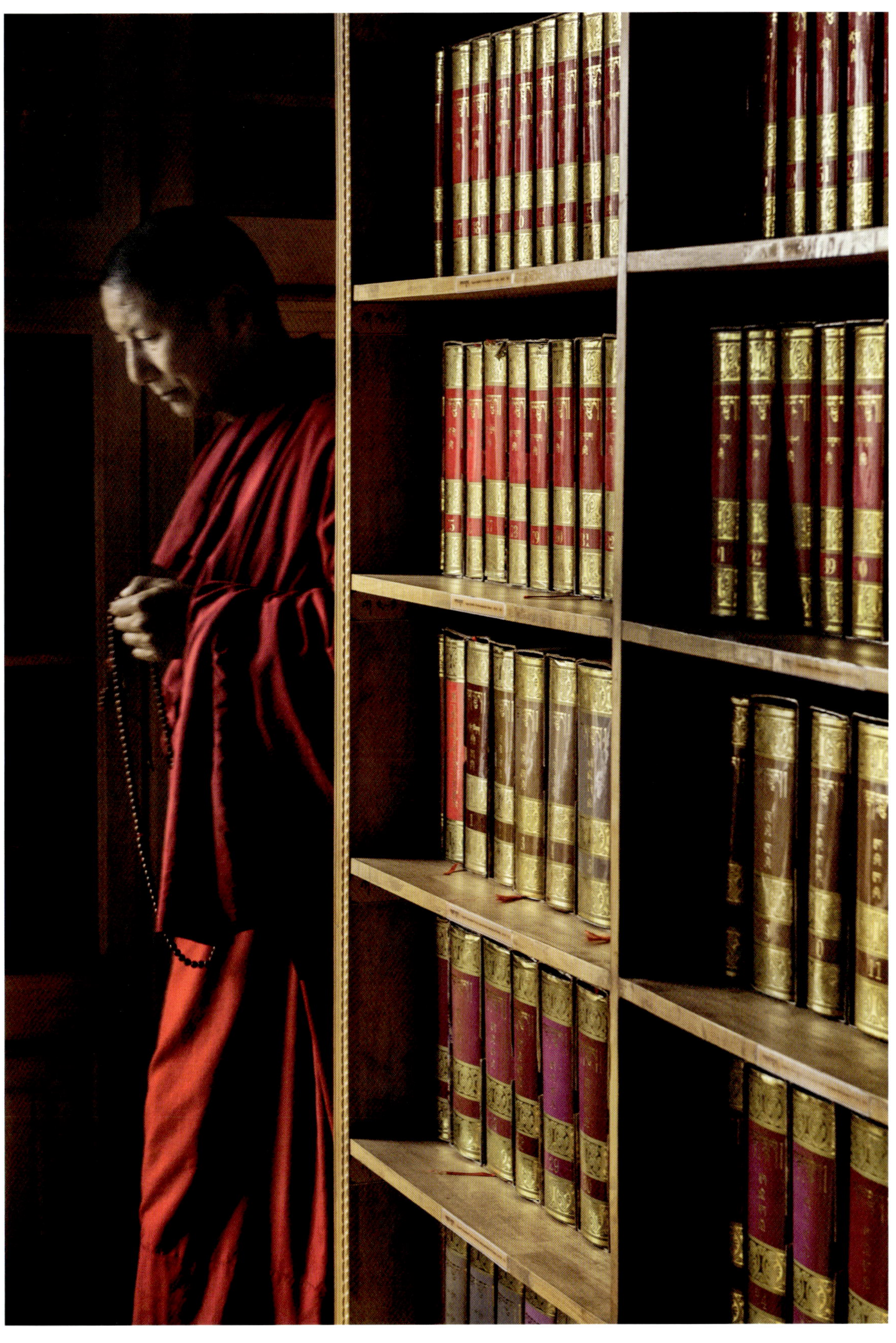

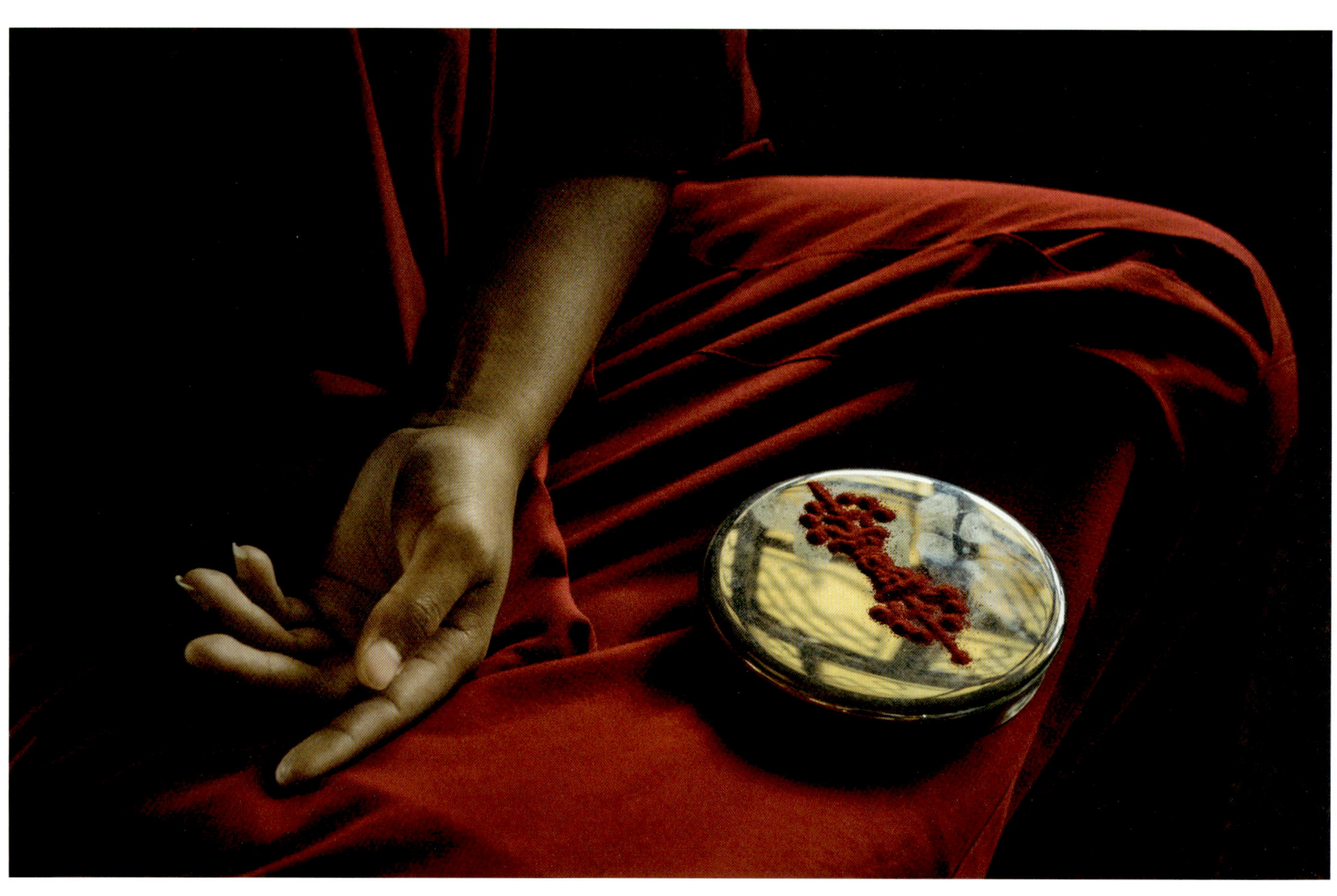

There can never be more than this moment.

Become free.

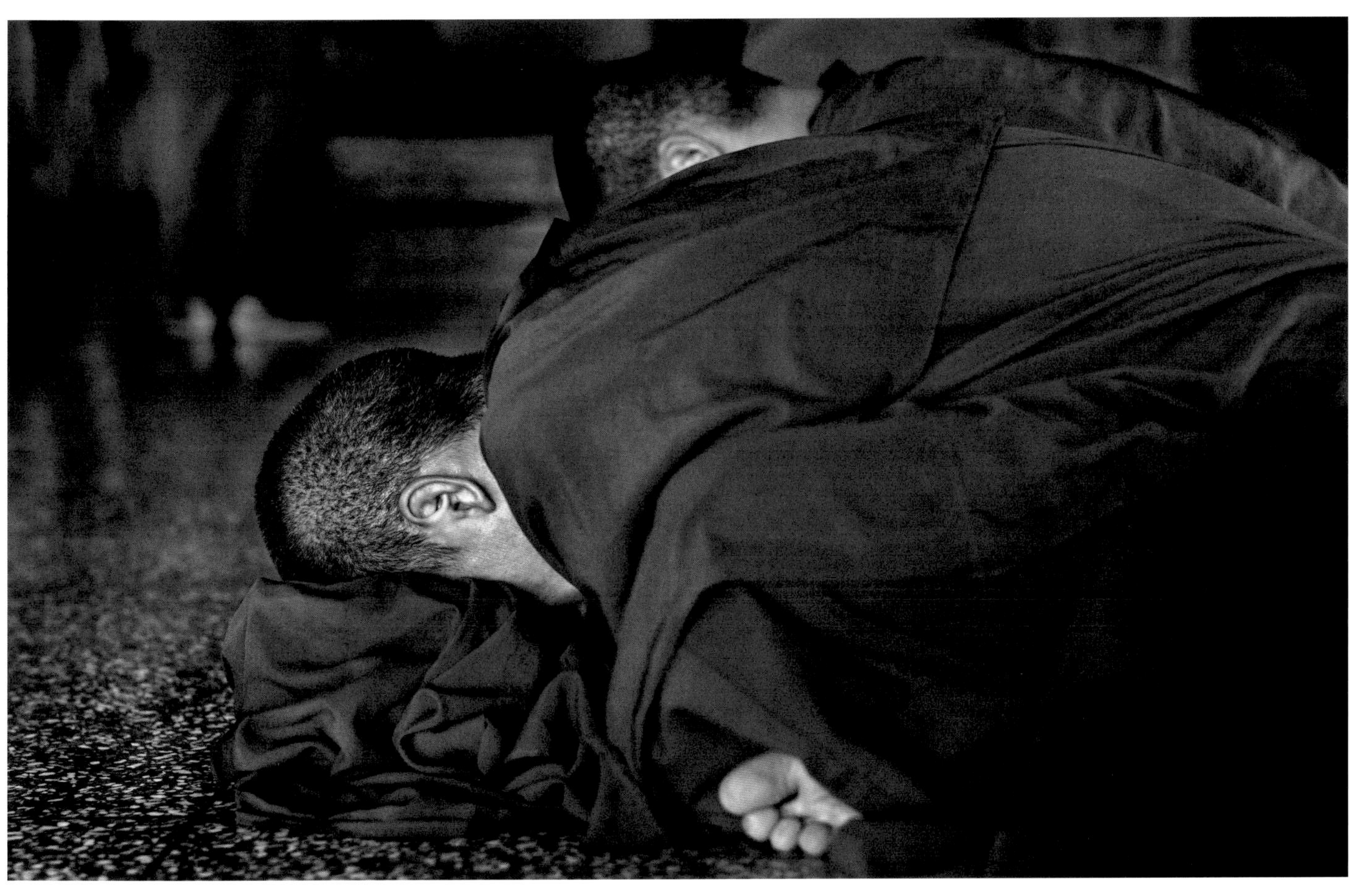

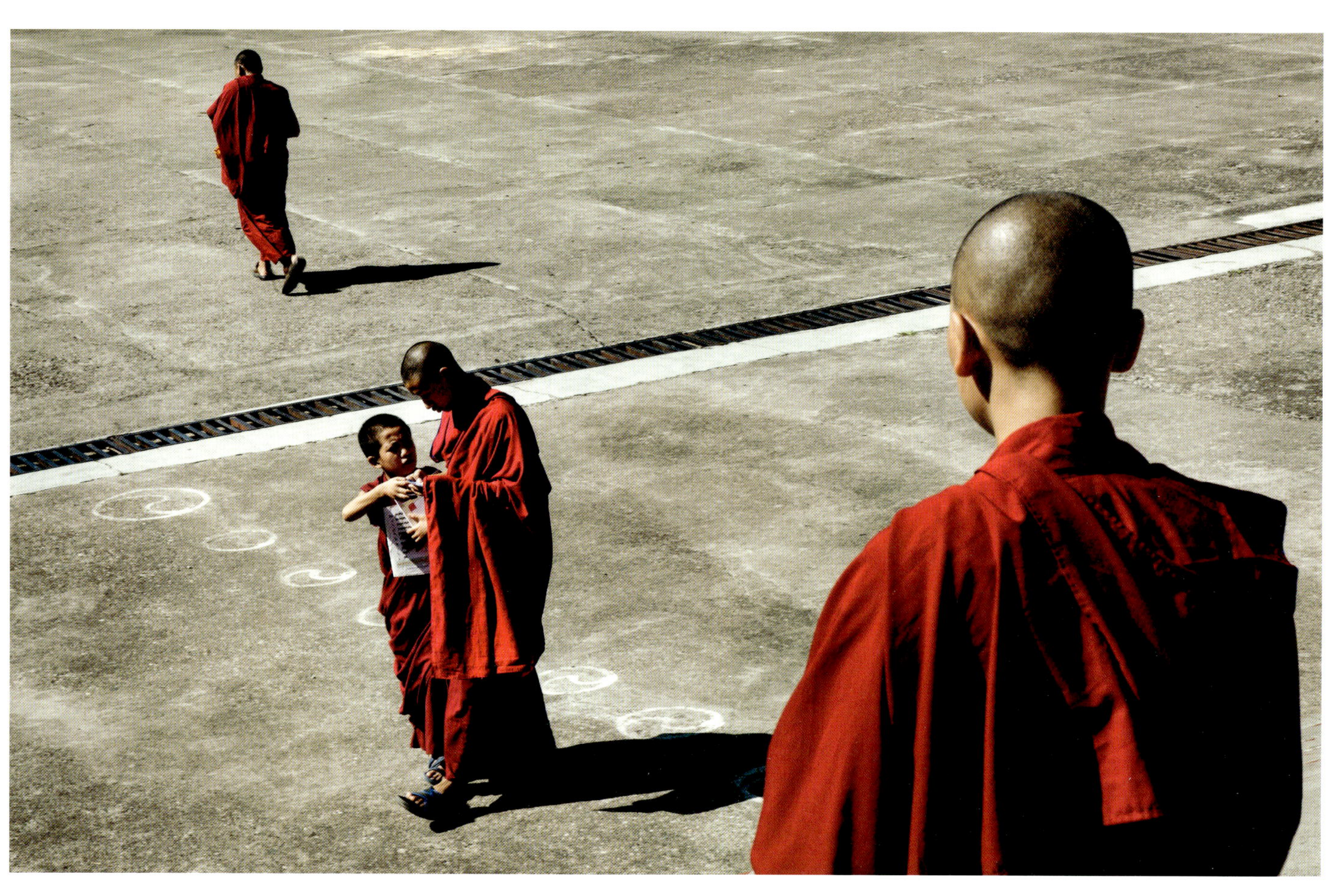

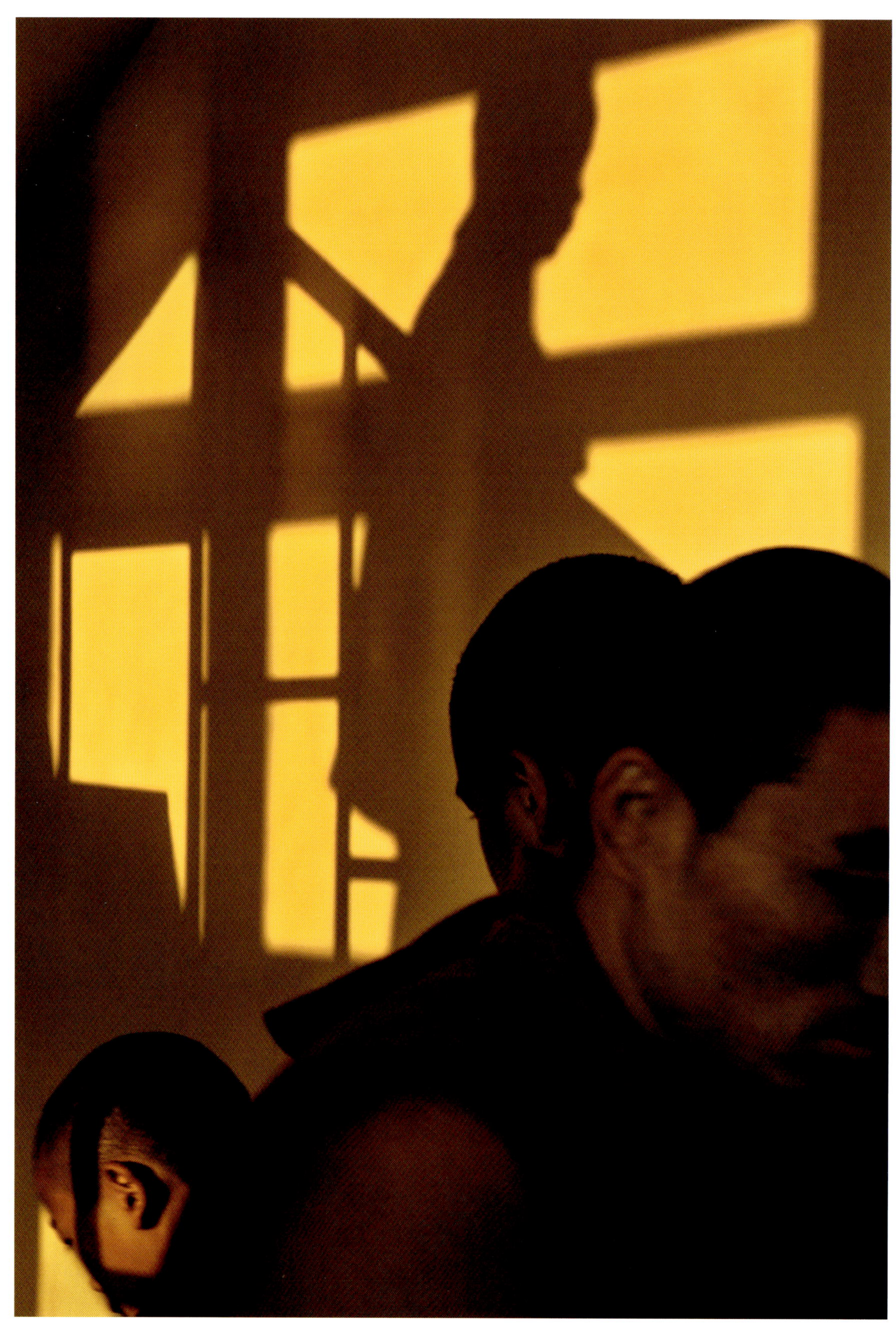

The Path of a Gyuto Monk

Entering at a young age, the first and deepest relationship formed is with their teacher. It's like a parent and child. It is their teacher who will shave their head and buy their first set of robes.

They are now a Pantsampa (primary school) having taken 36 vows and will study Tibetan and English and memorise the basic texts of philosophy.

At 17 or 18 years of age the monk moves to the main temple becoming a Getsul (high schooler) and there he focuses for the next 5 or 6 years on learning 500 pages of Buddhist texts, chanting and rituals. One of the most important of these rituals is the serving of tea in the temple which teaches respect. It is said that a Gyuto tea runner moves faster than a horse.

Full ordination including the taking of 253 vows takes the monk from Getsul to Gelong, the university phase, which deepens their studies and now includes the making of tormas (ritual offerings) and the sand mandala.

They are a big family which shares all the duties including the cooking and cleaning. Each new stage brings greater responsibility within the monastery. The final role that all monks must do is that of the Disciplinarian, a job which no one looks forward to.

The journey is long. Twenty to thirty years spent in the monastery is not considered long. It is a path of continuous study and not all will make it.

Student and Teacher

Students and teachers, children and parents. The bond is the same, it lasts a lifetime. The teacher guides the young monk and gives them their first robes.

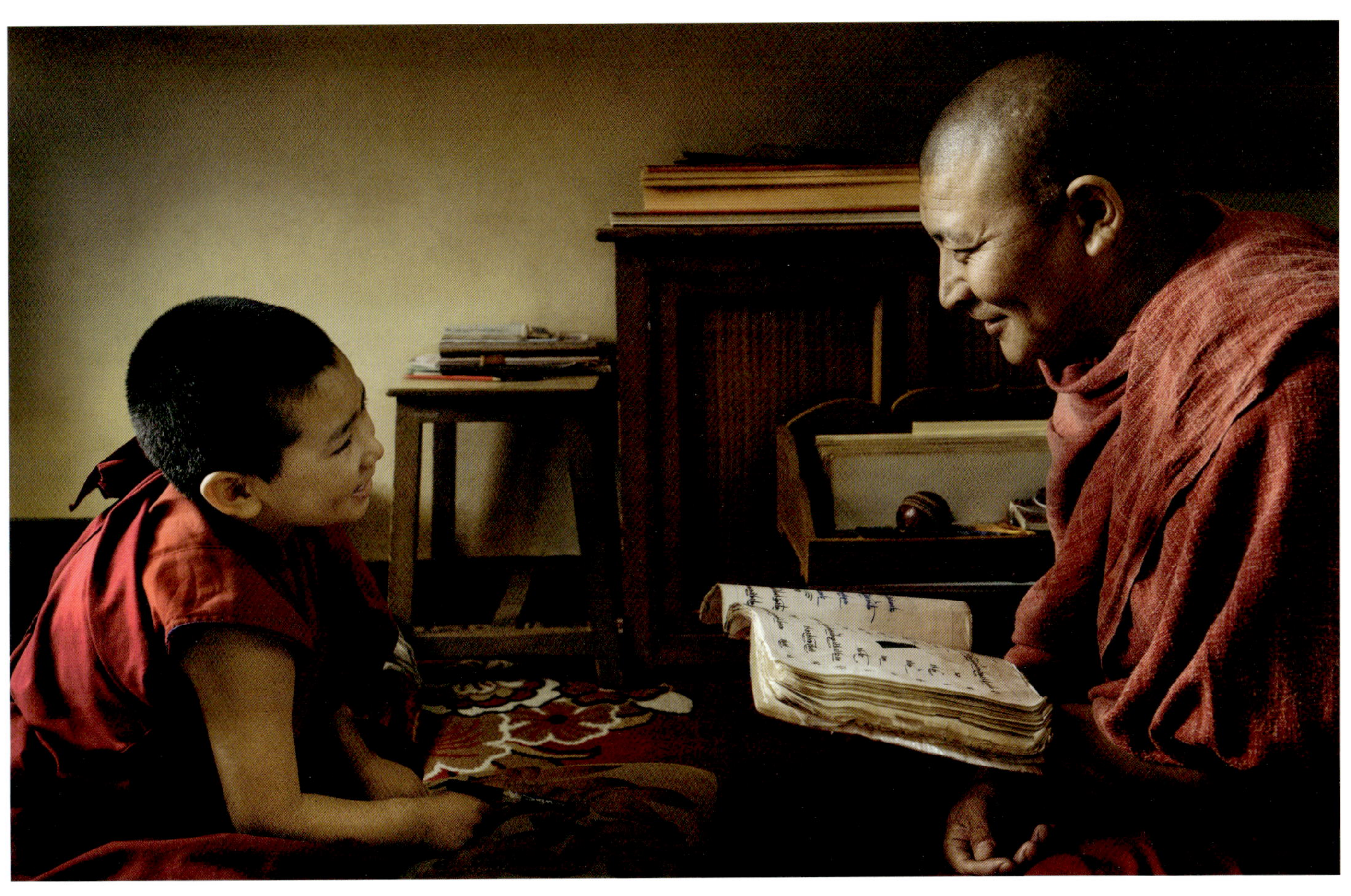

Non-attachment

The shaving of a monk's head is both a physical and symbolic cutting off of confusion, hostility and attachment.

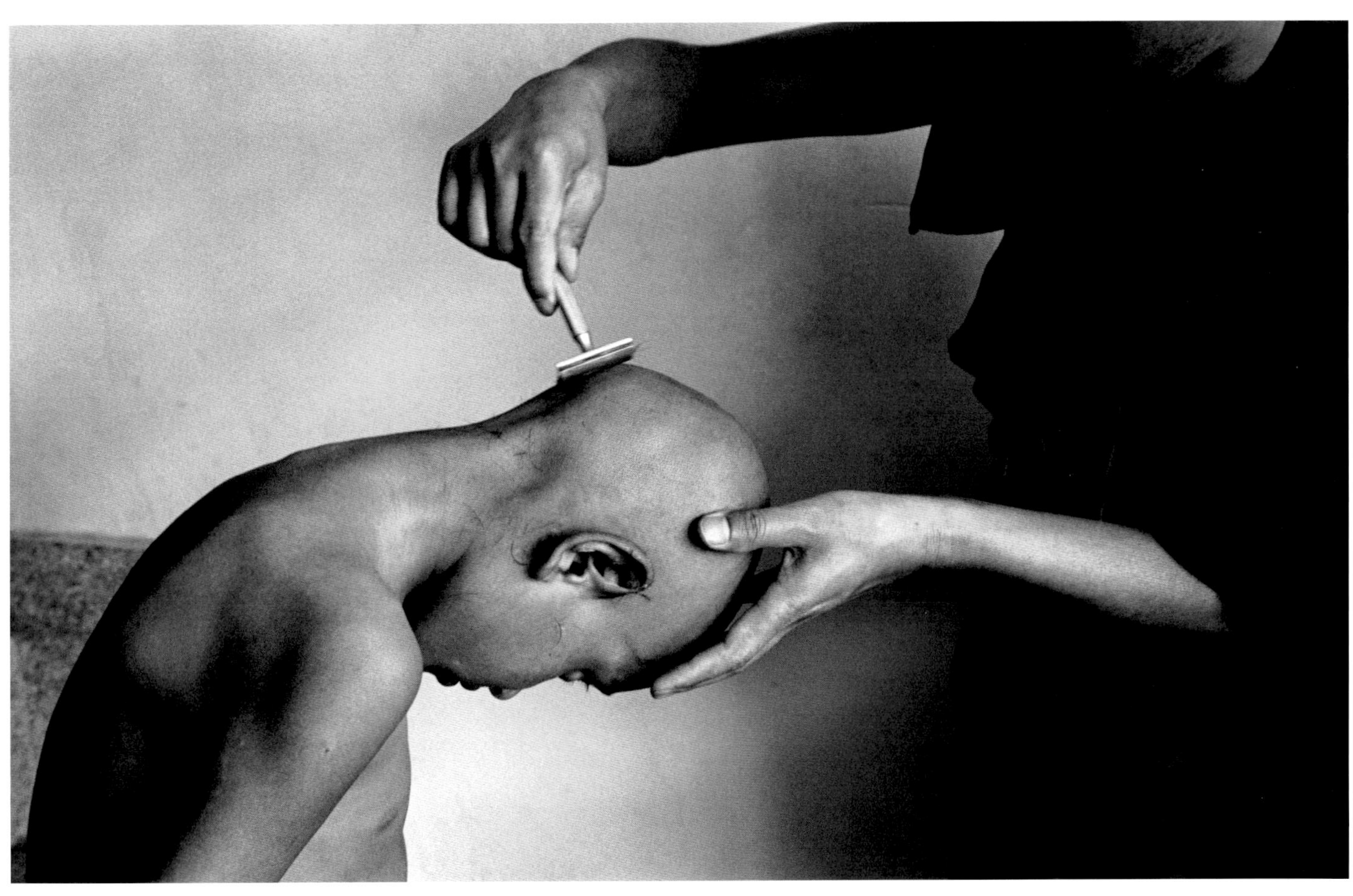

Vow

Many vows, Gelong, Getsul, Mantrayana vows and Bodhisattva vows. Vows are precepts, rules for monks which act as scaffolding for monastic life. A novice monk starts with 36 vows while a fully ordained monk takes 253 vows.

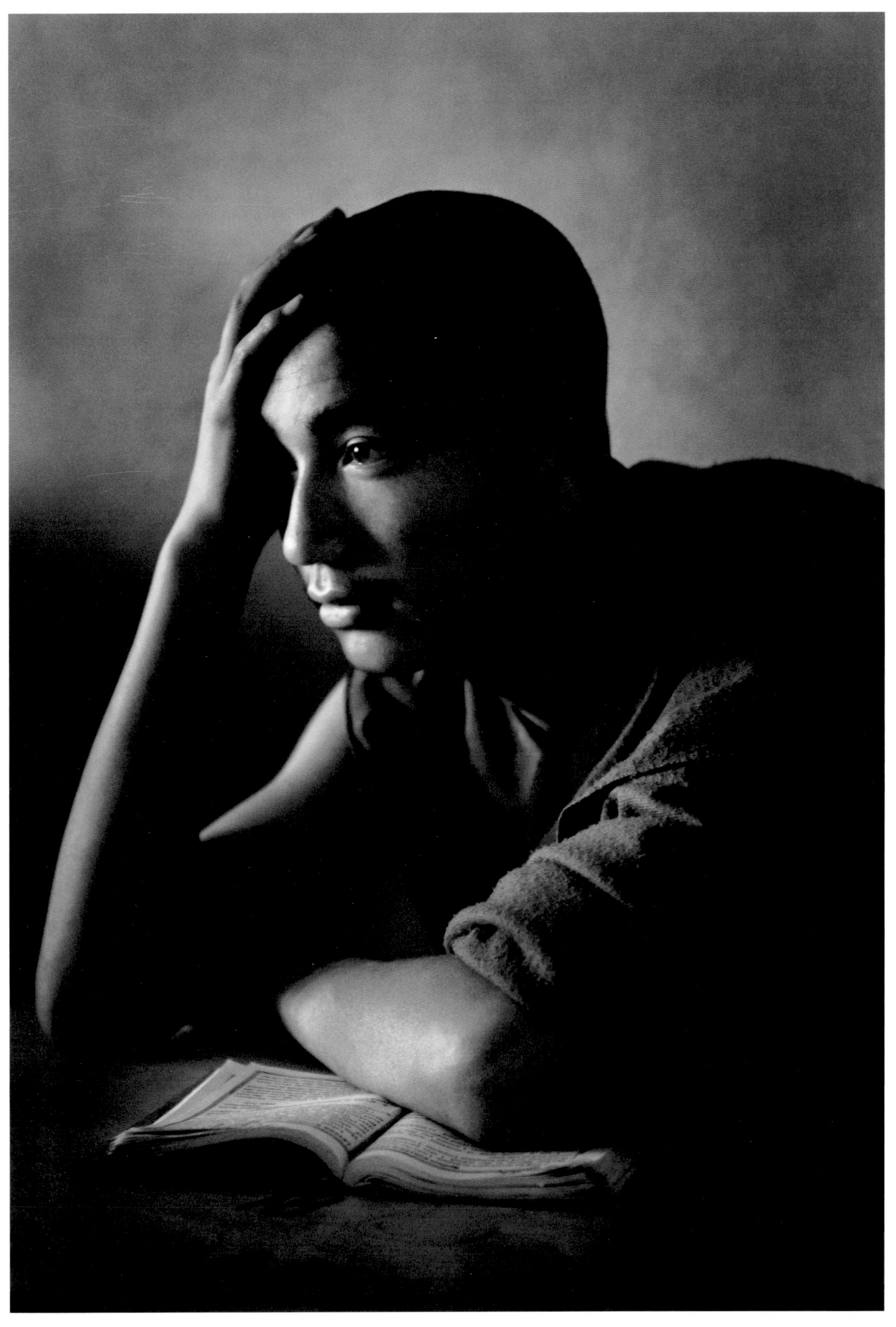

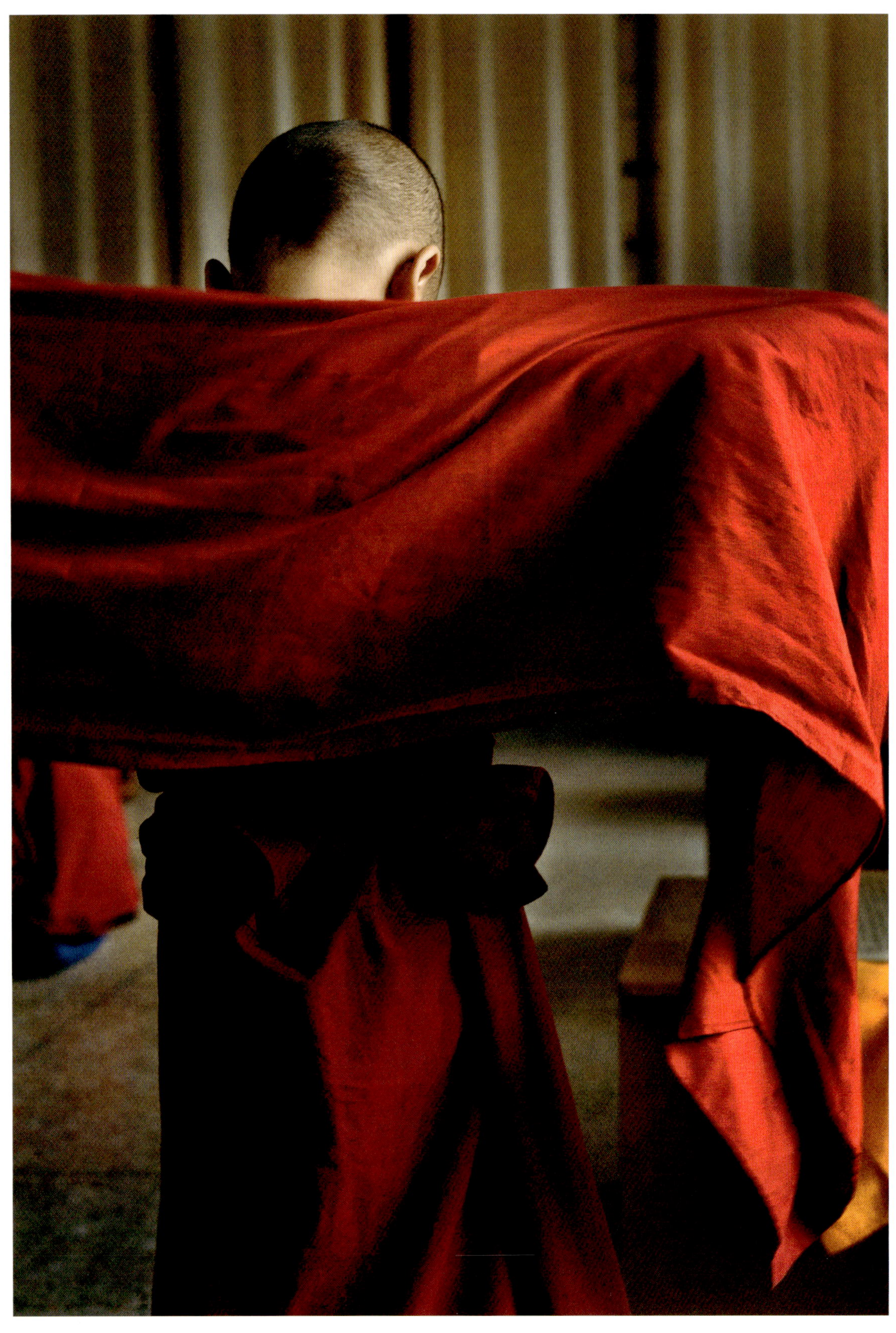

Pantsampa

Young monks often come with their parent's blessings from ages 6 to 8 years. All care for them is given by the monastery. They can choose to stay a monk or leave, it's their own choice. Freewill.

Teaching

The passing of information from master to student is an oral tradition. Teaching is an explanation of these words of the great masters, not simply a retelling of what they said.

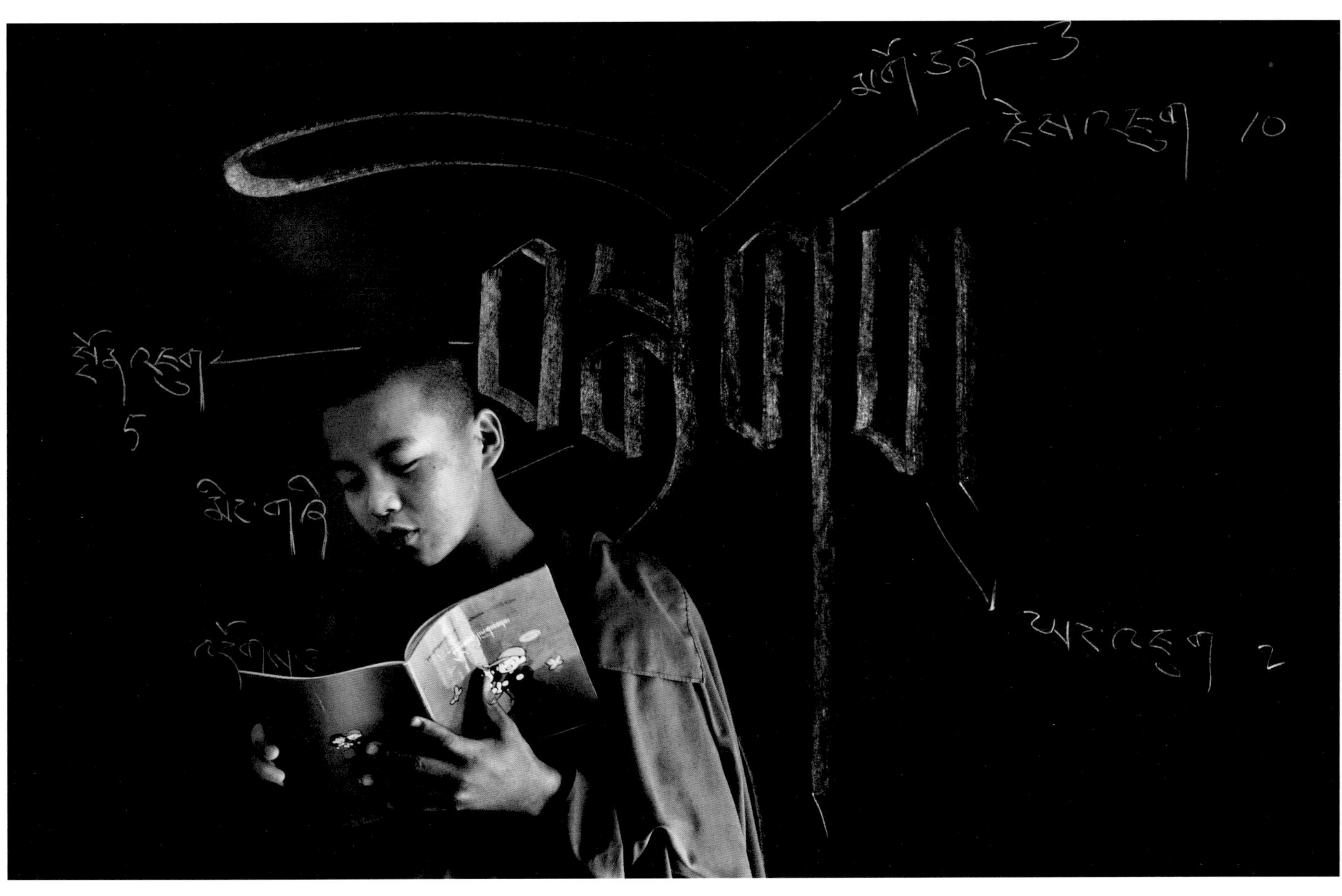

Study

Six thousand lines of tantric text must be learned verbatim. Tibetan grammar, calligraphy and English for the young. It is no ordinary curriculum, learning is food for the soul.

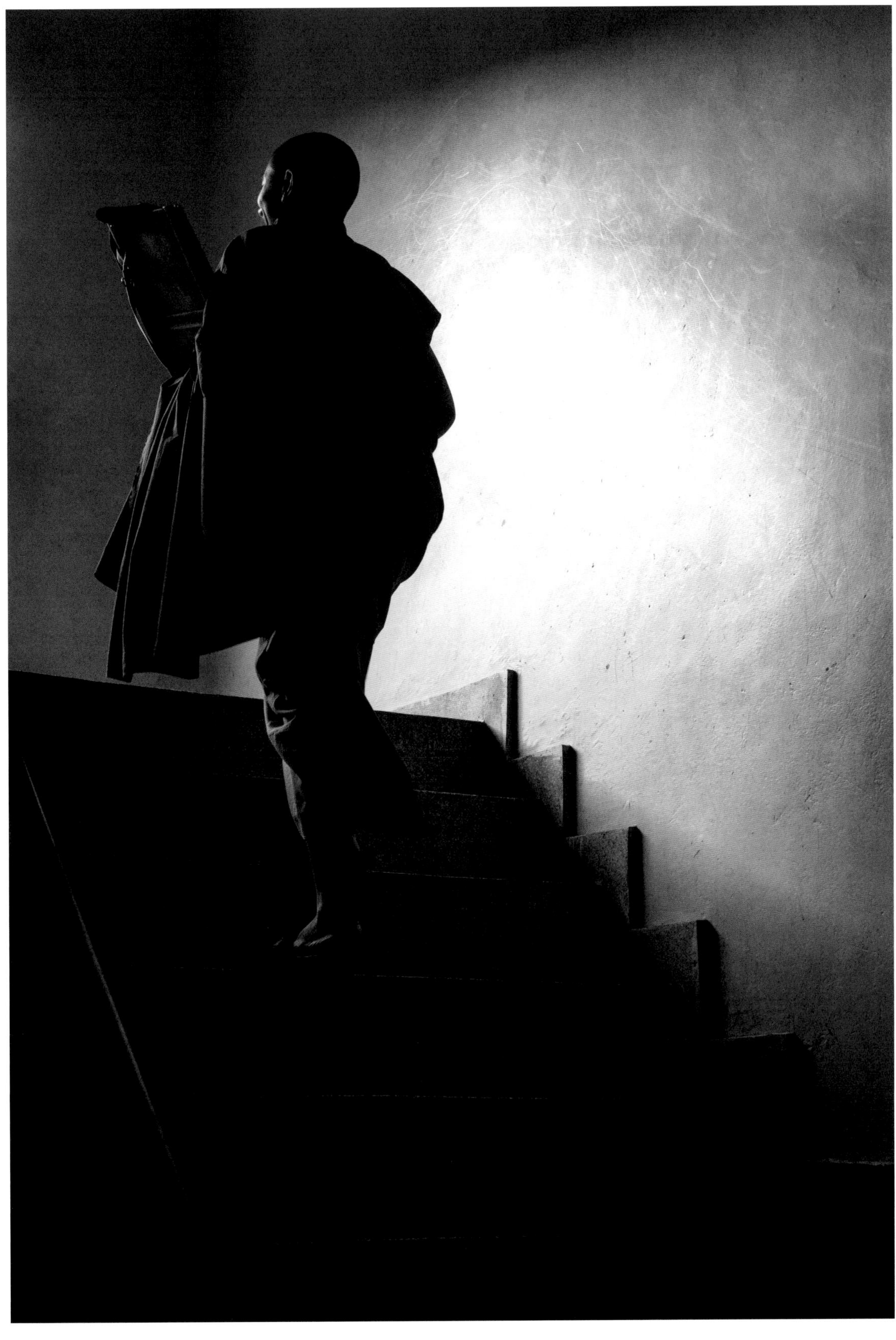

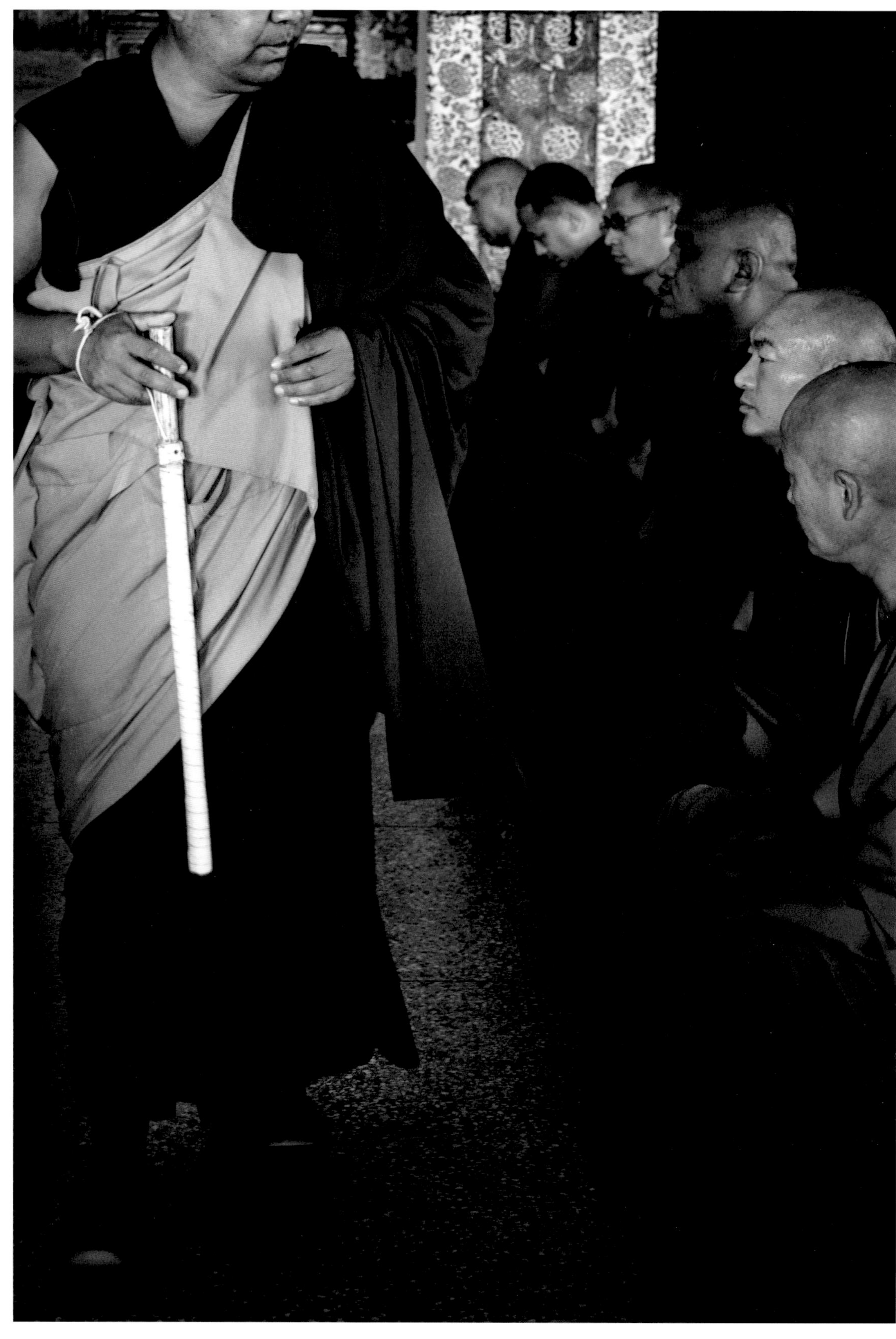

Discipline

The toughest and final duty within the monastery. Third in seniority after the Abbott and Vice-Abbott, the Disciplinarian is responsible for all monks following the rules. Each monk must do 6 months in this position.

Torma

A ritual offering to the Buddhas, Bodhisattvas and Deities during ceremonies. They are mostly sculpted butter and barley flour cakes. Each is made in specific shapes based upon their purpose.

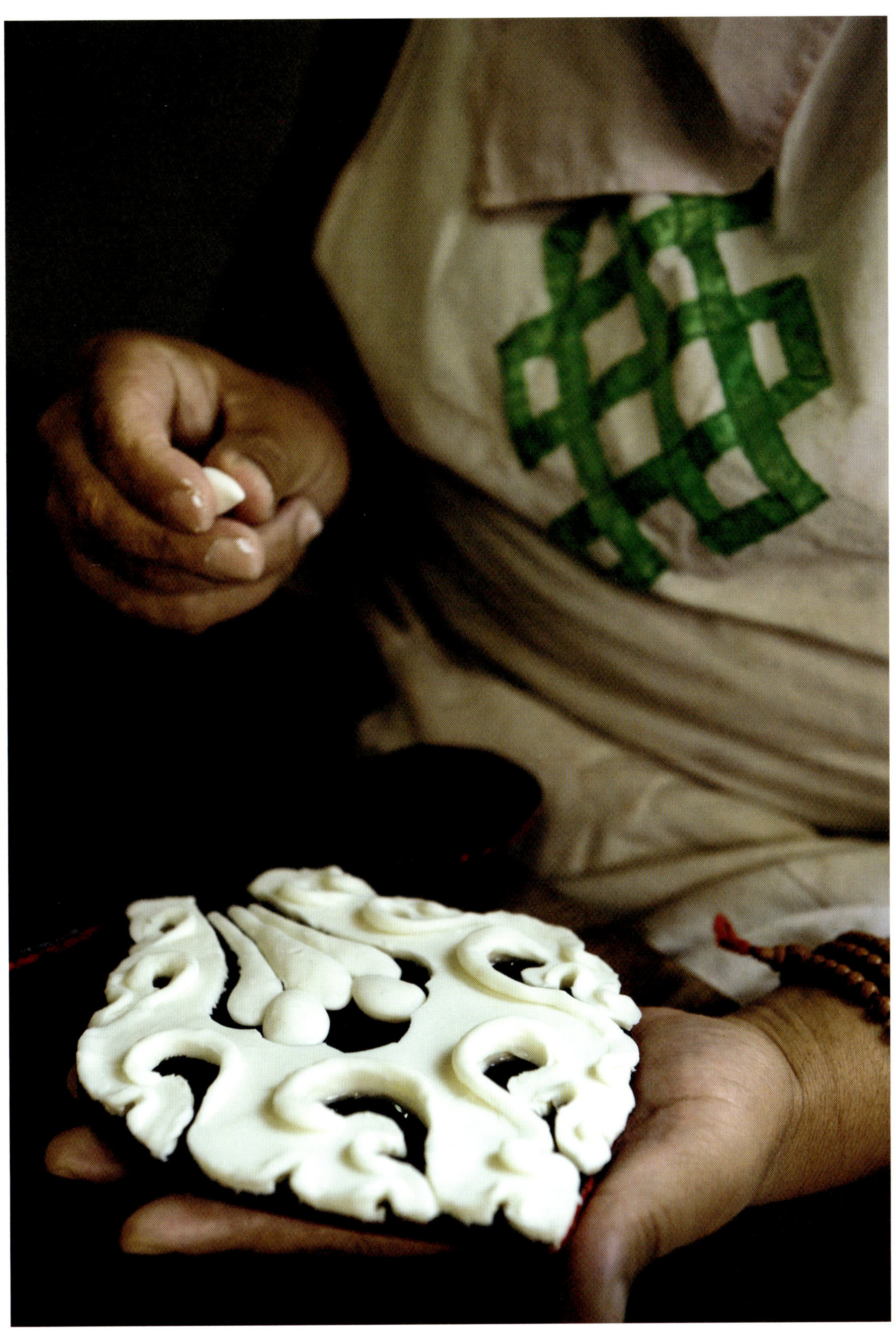

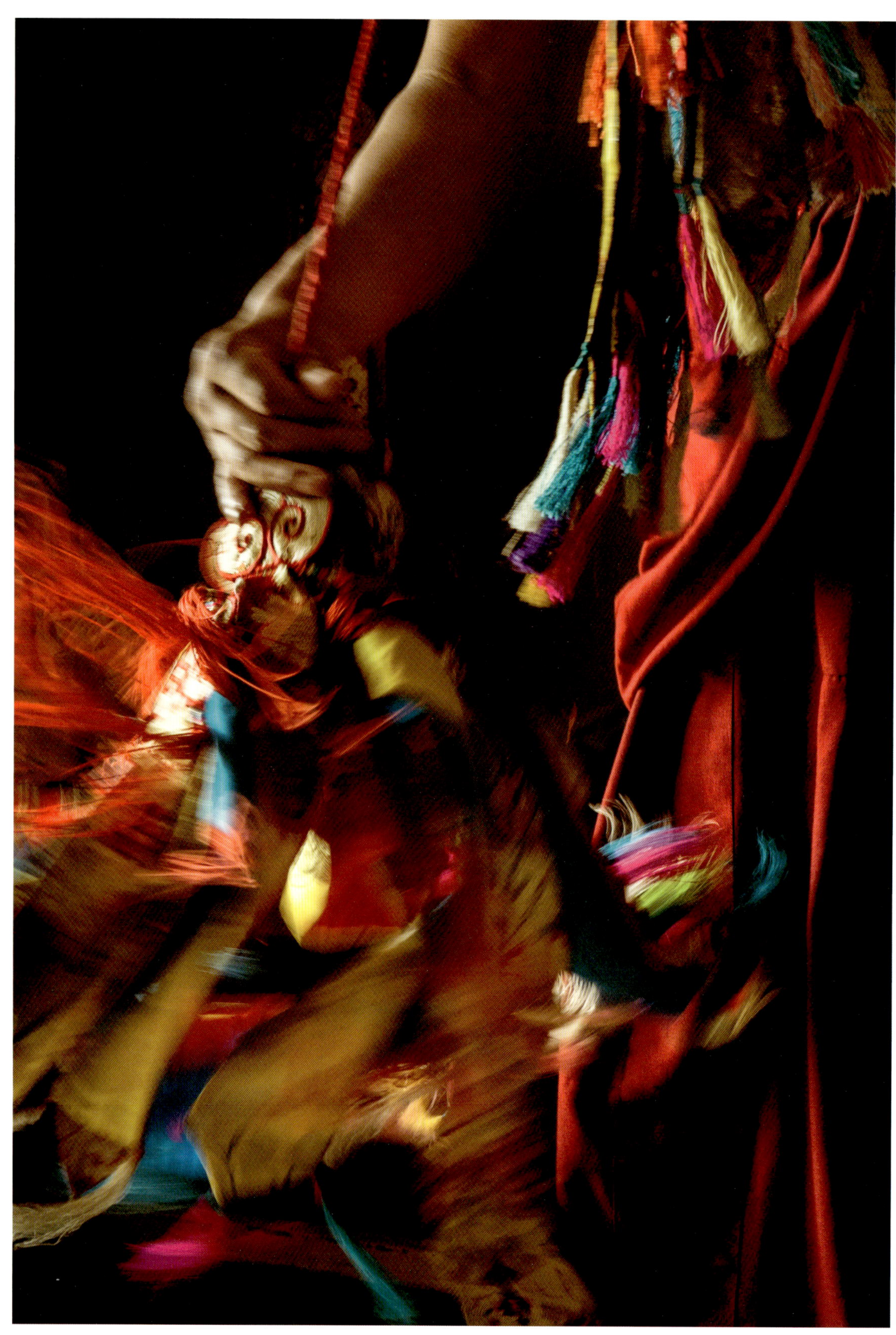

A Tantric Monastery

Two of the specialist tantric practices that the monks perform are the fire puja and the sand mandala. Beginners must receive initiation before they can perform them and each practise incorporates Tibetan deities and symbols via their intricate details.

The fire puja is part of the secret teachings and is offered at the end of special retreats and at certain times throughout the year. Each item burnt during the puja has a specific purpose and the potential to affect your life (grains pacify sickness, crepe grass for longevity and butter for wealth).

There are 4 types of fire pujas: Pacifying (calms sickness), Increasing (prolongs life, wealth, wisdom), Controlling (over people in order to benefit them), Wrathful (used only when others don't work and can only be done with strong compassion and pure morality).

The monastery creates 3 different types of mandalas. A mandala can be created in sand, wood or as a painting, but it is first practiced and learnt in clay. Mandala, meaning circle, represents a perfectly harmonious world, a pure universe.

The monks use the construction of it as a meditative practice. It is believed that the creation of the mandala transmits positive energies to the environment and to those who view them. After completion it is ceremoniously destroyed. The underlying message of this ritual is non-attachment and impermanence.

The sand is then swept up and dispersed into flowing water as a way of extending the healing powers to the world.

Tea Ceremony

*Younger monks serve tea. It develops respect and
is a tour of duty. All monks come through this way.*

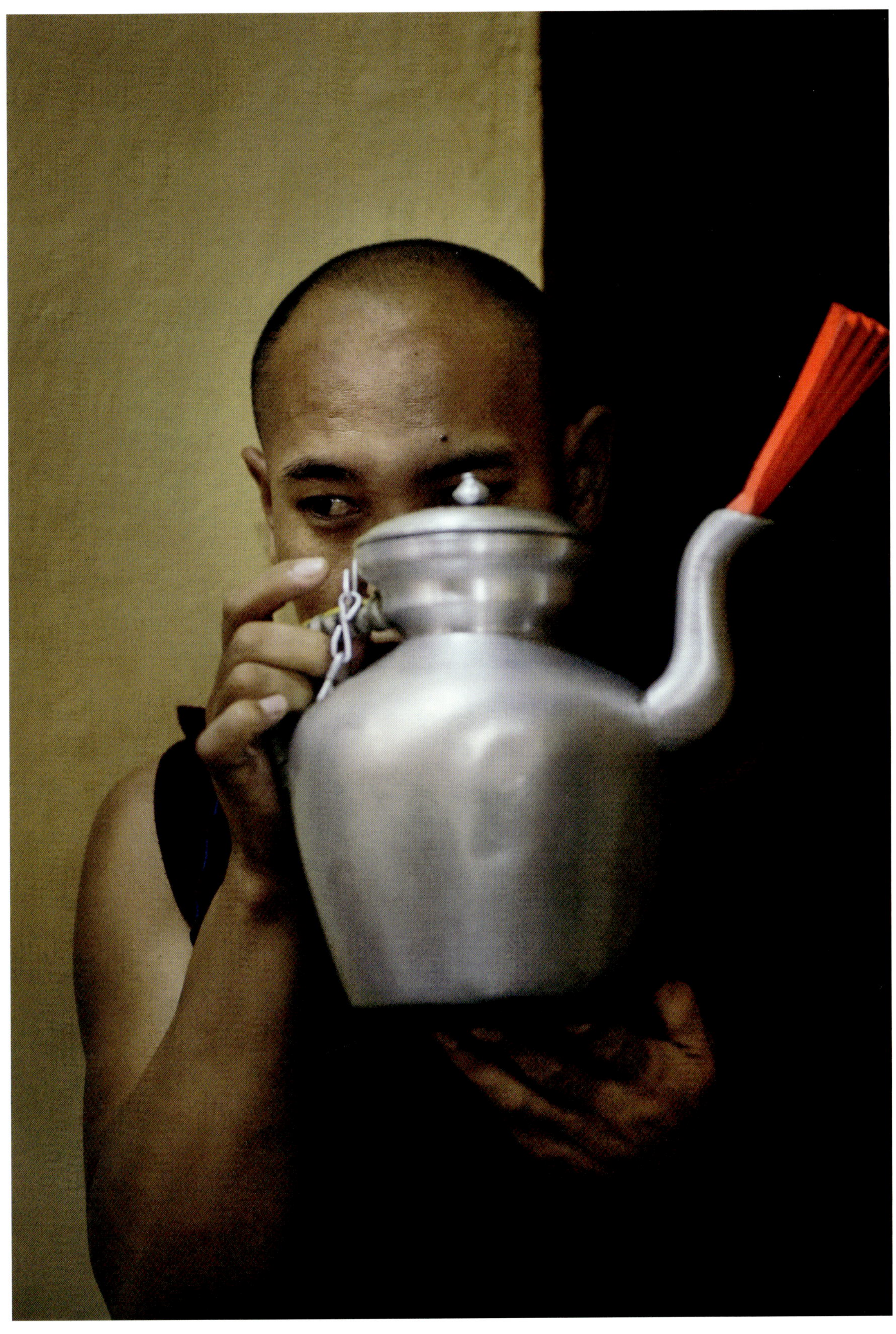

Chanting

*Chanting to meditate, to embody the teachings and
to experience them in a way that the mind cannot.*

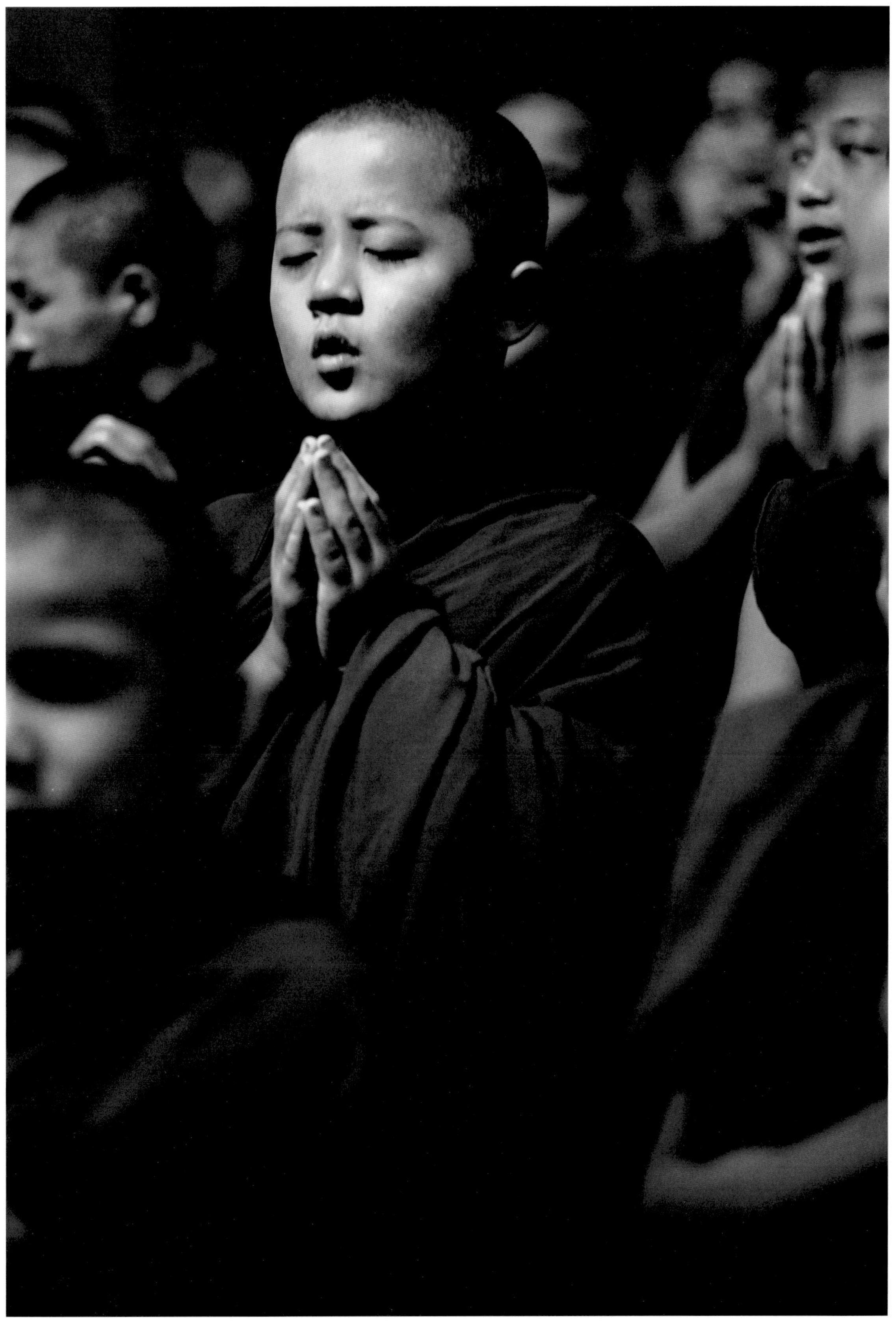

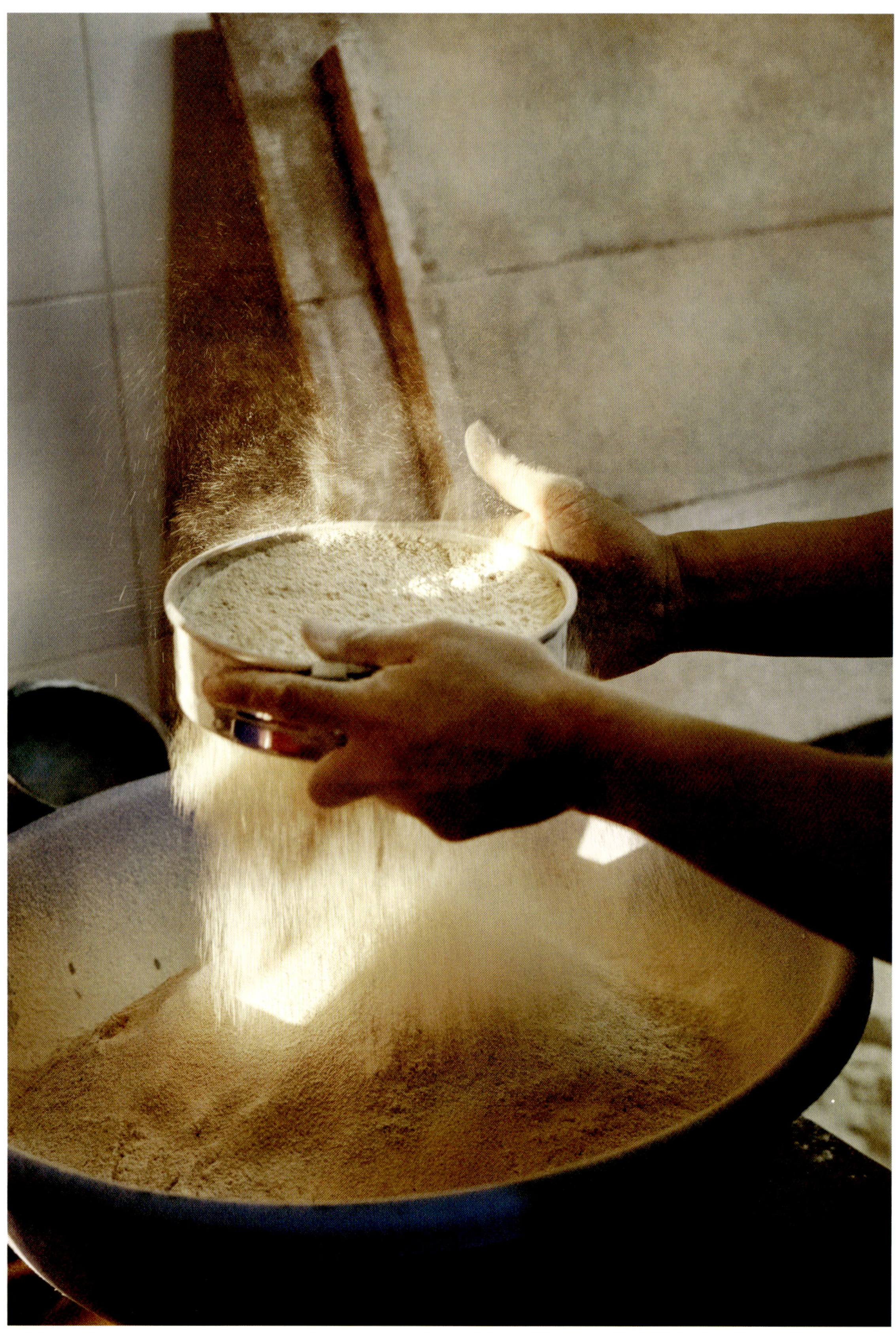

Ritual

Rituals are the bedrock of monastery life. Chanting, shaving heads, making tormas, sand mandalas, butter sculptures and pujas. The swirl of the daily happenings of the monastery.

Task

Duties in the monastery underpin the workings of this vast commune. Everyone rotates through these tasks which include pujas, cooking, ritual preparations, cleaning, teaching the younger monks, serving tea and temple caretaker among many others.

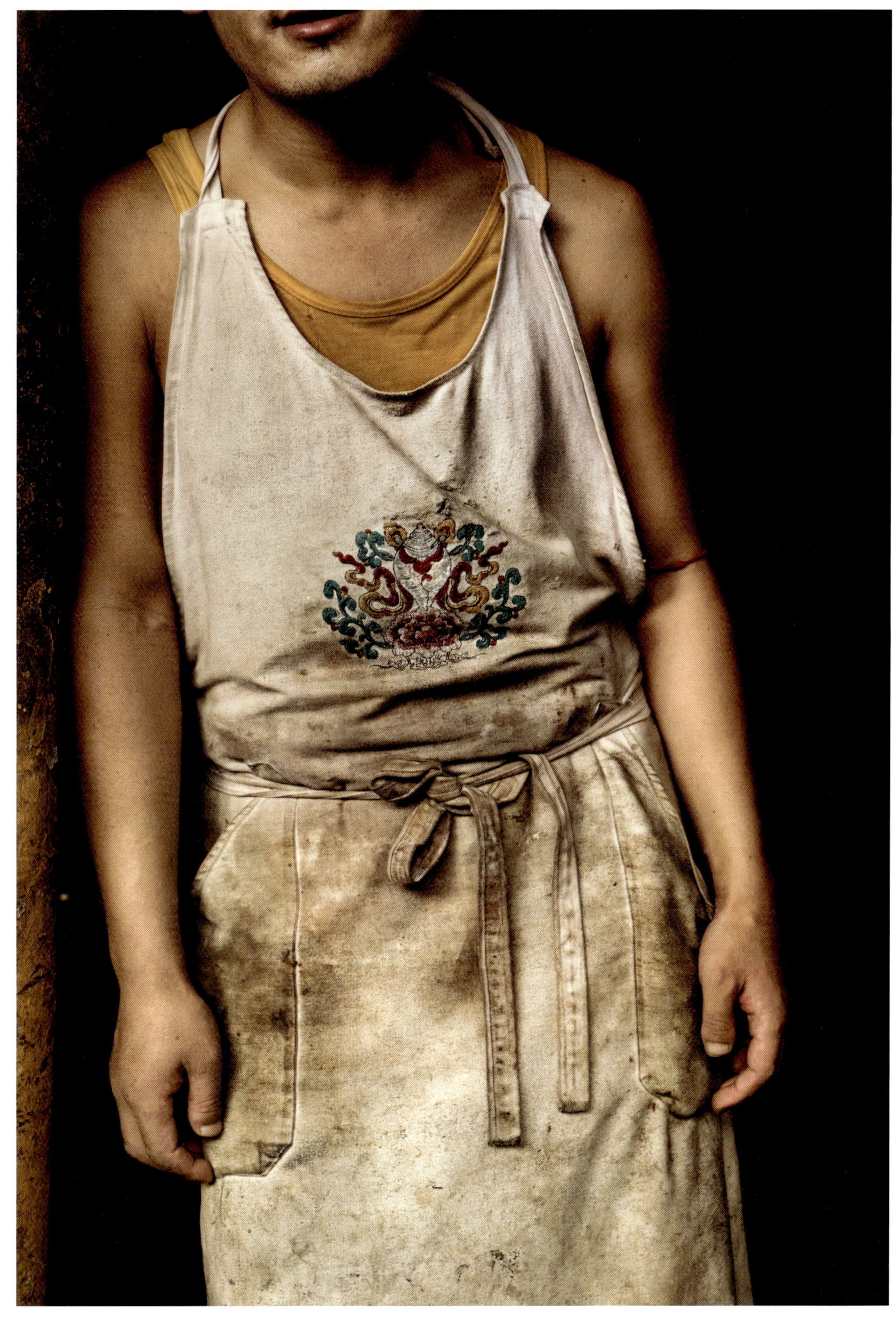

Kitchen

From 4am each day ten people, both monks and lay people, prepare and cook for all of the monastery. Over 400 pieces of bread are made fresh daily. As part of their duties all monks spend some time serving in the kitchen.

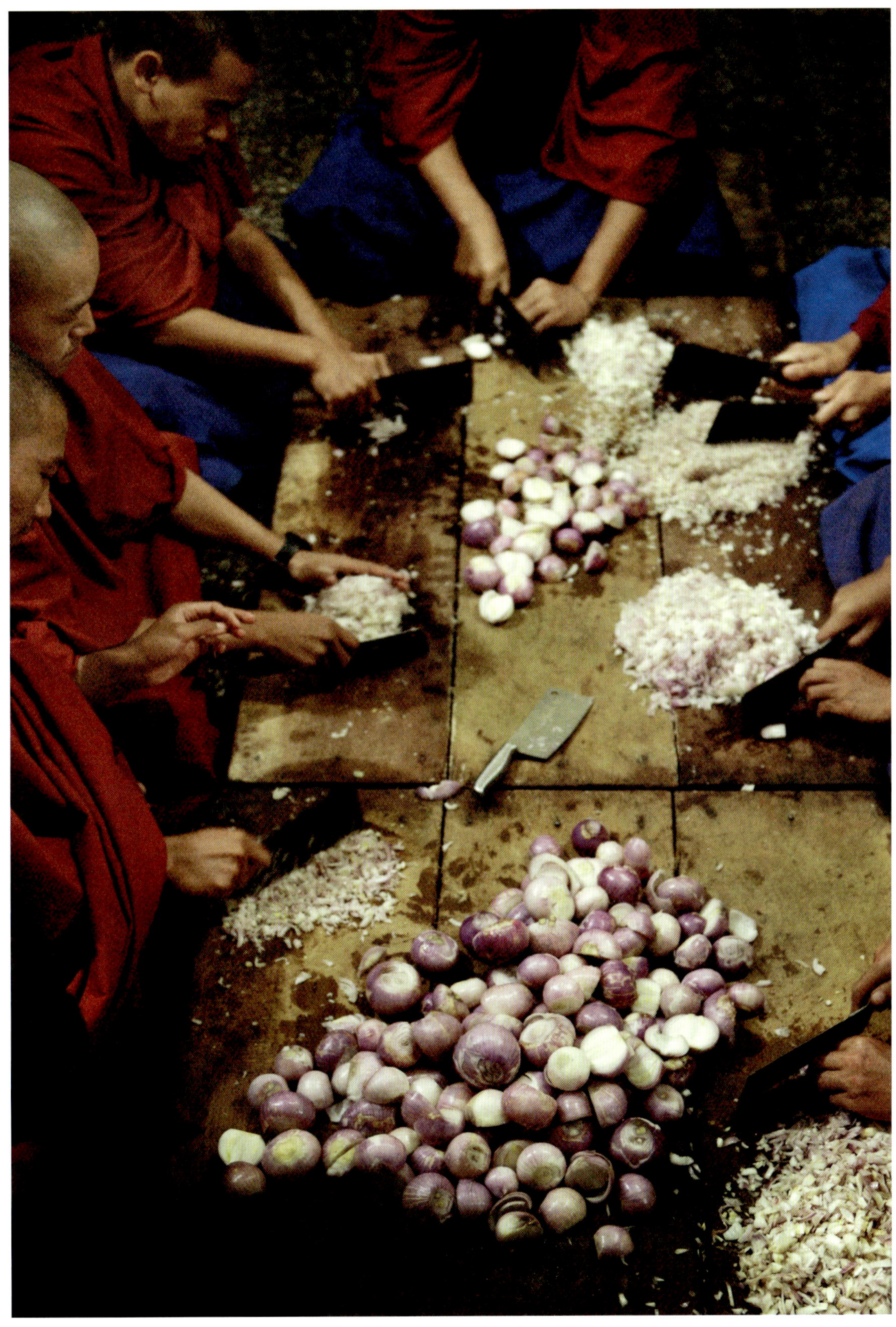

Retreat

A solitary time. Retreats can be 3 years, 2 months or a single week. An opportunity for intensive contemplation and self realisation practices.

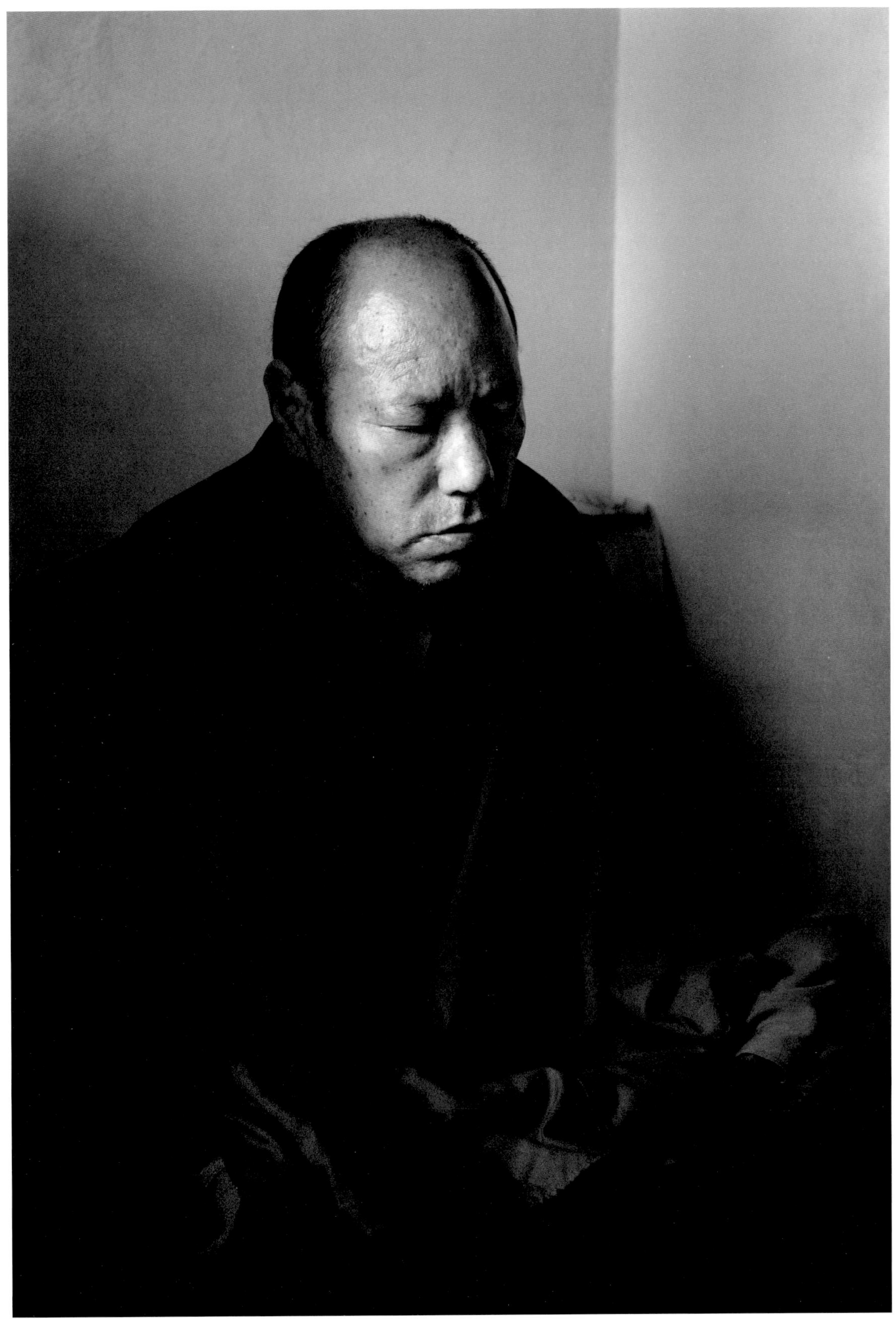

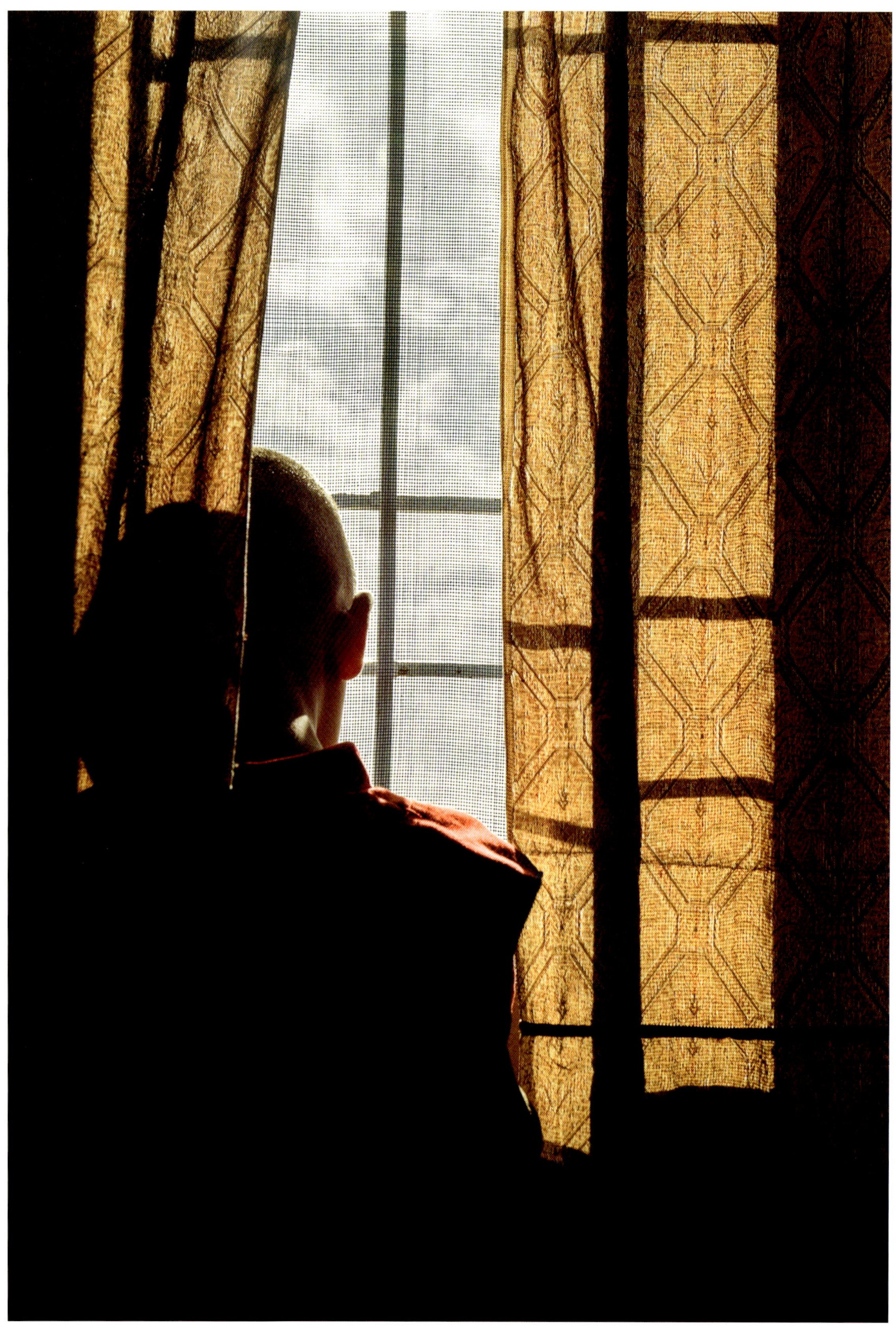

Meditation

From the outside it can all look the same but there are differences. Contemplative for stabilising, analytical for focusing on the"chattering monkey mind." Both use the same concepts of emptiness, Bodhicitta and selflessness.

Yellow Hat

Yellow for higher training. Each string in the arch represents the thousand Buddhas that will come to earth. The arch sitting upon the head embodies the gesture of bowing in respect to the Buddhas.

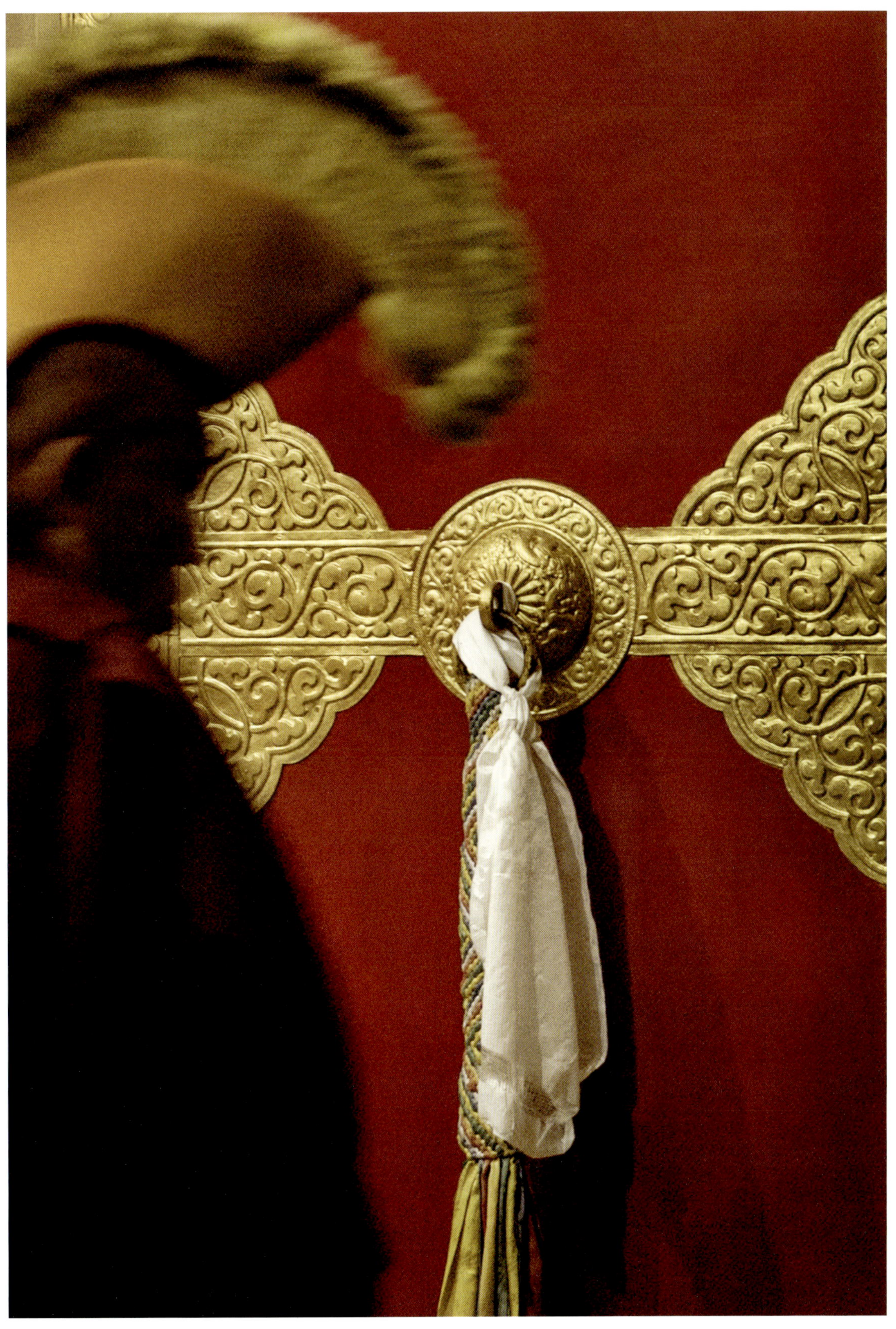

Prayer Ceremonies

In Tibetan these are called "Pujas" and are used to remove obstacles in order to help in areas of sickness, dying and death or to help create success in other areas of life.

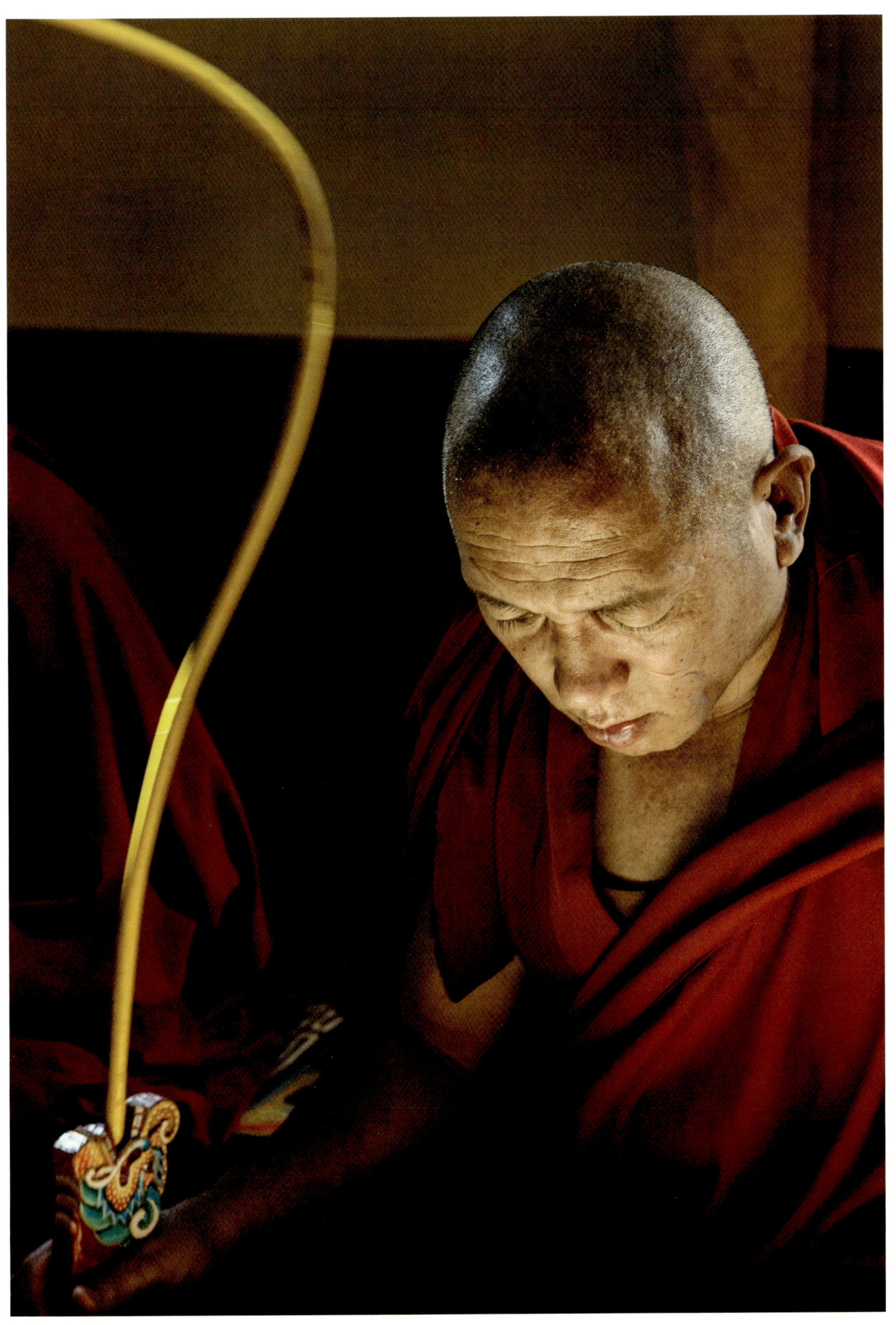

Ceremonial Objects

Tantric ceremonies need three important ritual objects. A Bell and Dorjee representing the inseparability of wisdom and emptiness and a Skull Cup or Kapala, used as an offering bowl which may contain dough cakes or wine to be offered to the deities during the puja.

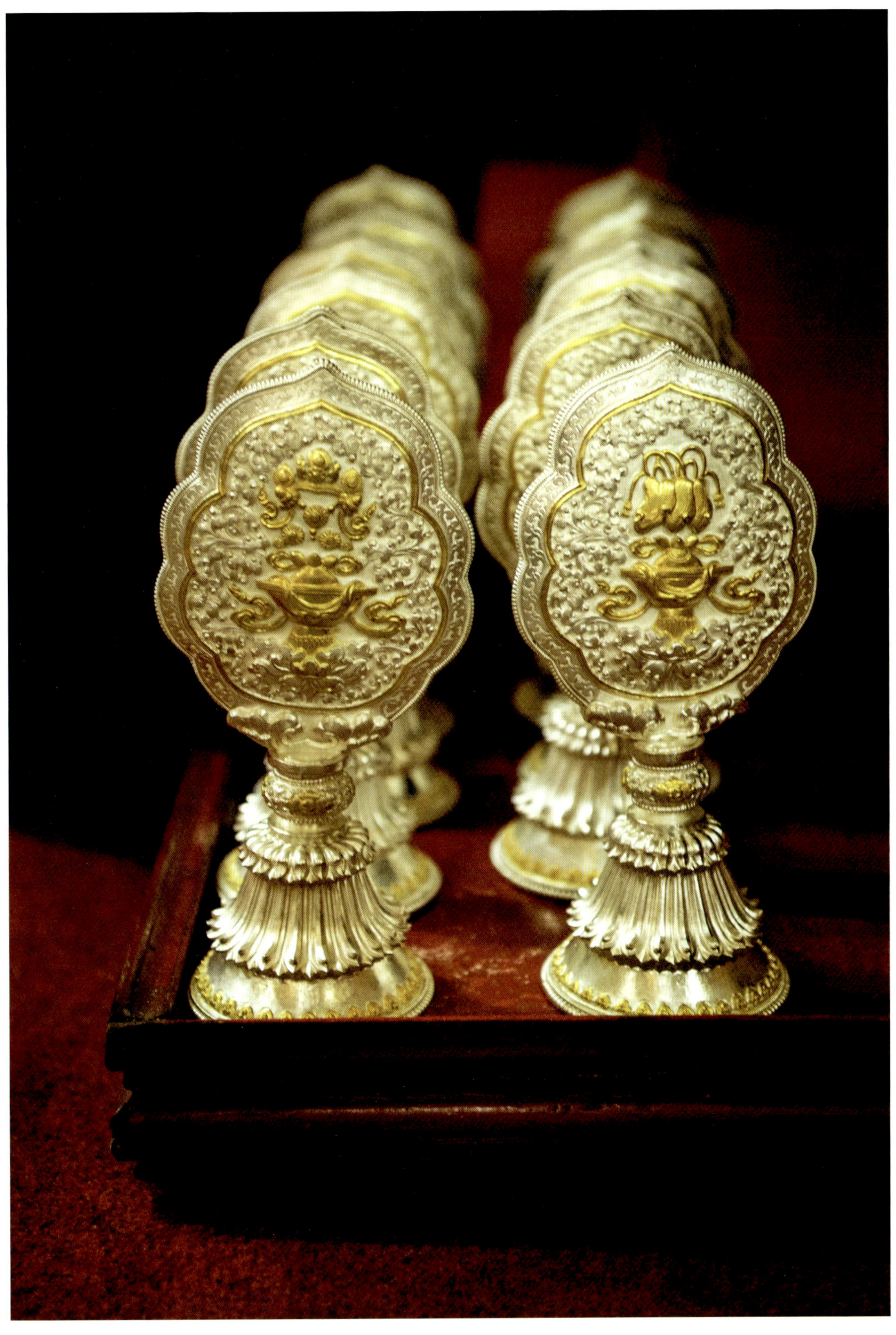

Being

They are together, as one, a community and a family. The monastery is their home, sacred and nurturing, like many brothers under the one roof. Practicing and studying.

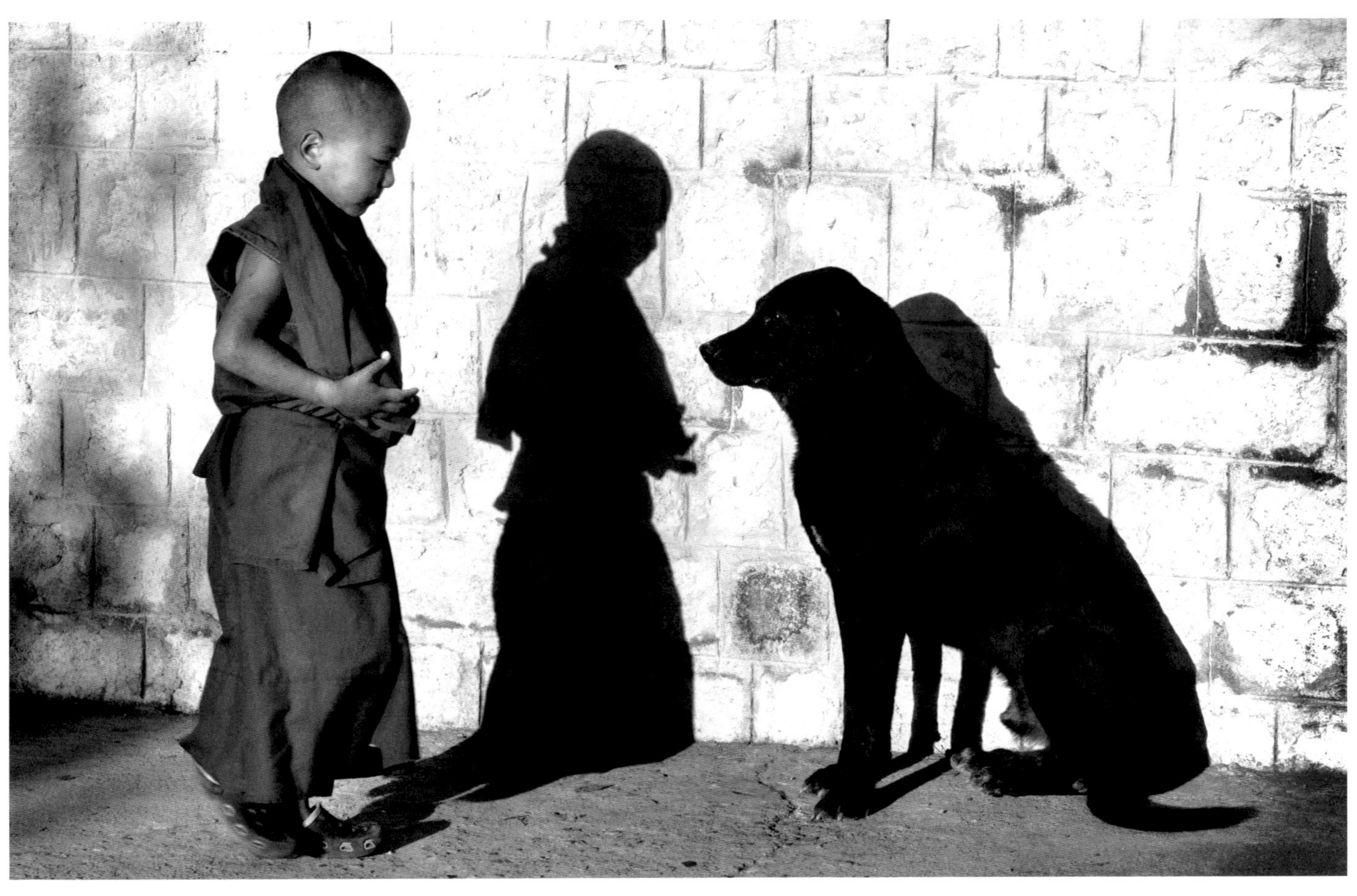

Diaspora

As Buddhism developed in Tibet, four lineages grew based upon specific teachings, different interpretations and different locations. The last of these is the Gelug lineage, pioneered by the great saint scholar Tsongkhapa who revitalised and reformed the practice of sutra and tantra.

Tantrism refers to a specific approach or type of practice which has the connotation of an esoteric system in which the practices and rituals are handed down directly from the teacher to their students by word of mouth. Tsongkhapa's tradition of tantric teaching was mainly established in the tantric monasteries of Gyudmed and Gyuto.

From its inception in 1474 the Gyuto Monastery served as the greatest place of Buddhist esoteric teachings through its calendar of regular and special activities. Strict discipline was observed and its unique monastic traditions were maintained and handed on with great care. Its system and tradition of tantric ritual spread to thousands of monasteries within Tibet, Mongolia, Ladhak and other neighbouring countries.

The monastery, which began with thirty-two monks, grew to between eight and nine hundred monks over the last few centuries. But in 1959 due to the Chinese invasion and atrocities, only about sixty monks were able to escape to India as refugees. The rest were either killed in bombardments or captured and imprisoned in concentration camps. The temple, its sacred antiquities and most of the priceless images in it were destroyed.

The few monks who managed to flee to India initially settled in Dalhousie in the north western foothills of the Himalayas where they started a small handicrafts centre to maintain themselves. Between working hours they tried to perform all their religious activities and keep alive their traditional teachings and practices. As their material position improved they began to admit a few new monks each year to keep the monastery alive.

In 1974, on the advice to the Council of Religious Affair of His Holiness the Dalai Lama, the monastery moved to a Tibetan settlement in Tenzin Gang in the eastern state of Arunachal Pradesh, Assam India as part of a land settlement project.

The land was mainly used for orchards and vegetable growing. Workers were hired to do the cultivation so that the monks could devote more time to study and practice. Thus, but for a few exceptions, most of the regular religious activities were performed in accordance with the traditions that had been followed in Tibet.

The number of resident monks has now grown to over five hundred. The younger monks receive some modern education including English, Tibetan, arithmetic, general studies and other subjects in addition to their normal monastic education. Several monks have been appointed to look after the financial interests of the monastery in different places in an attempt to make the monastery self-supporting.

Gyuto Tantric Monastery

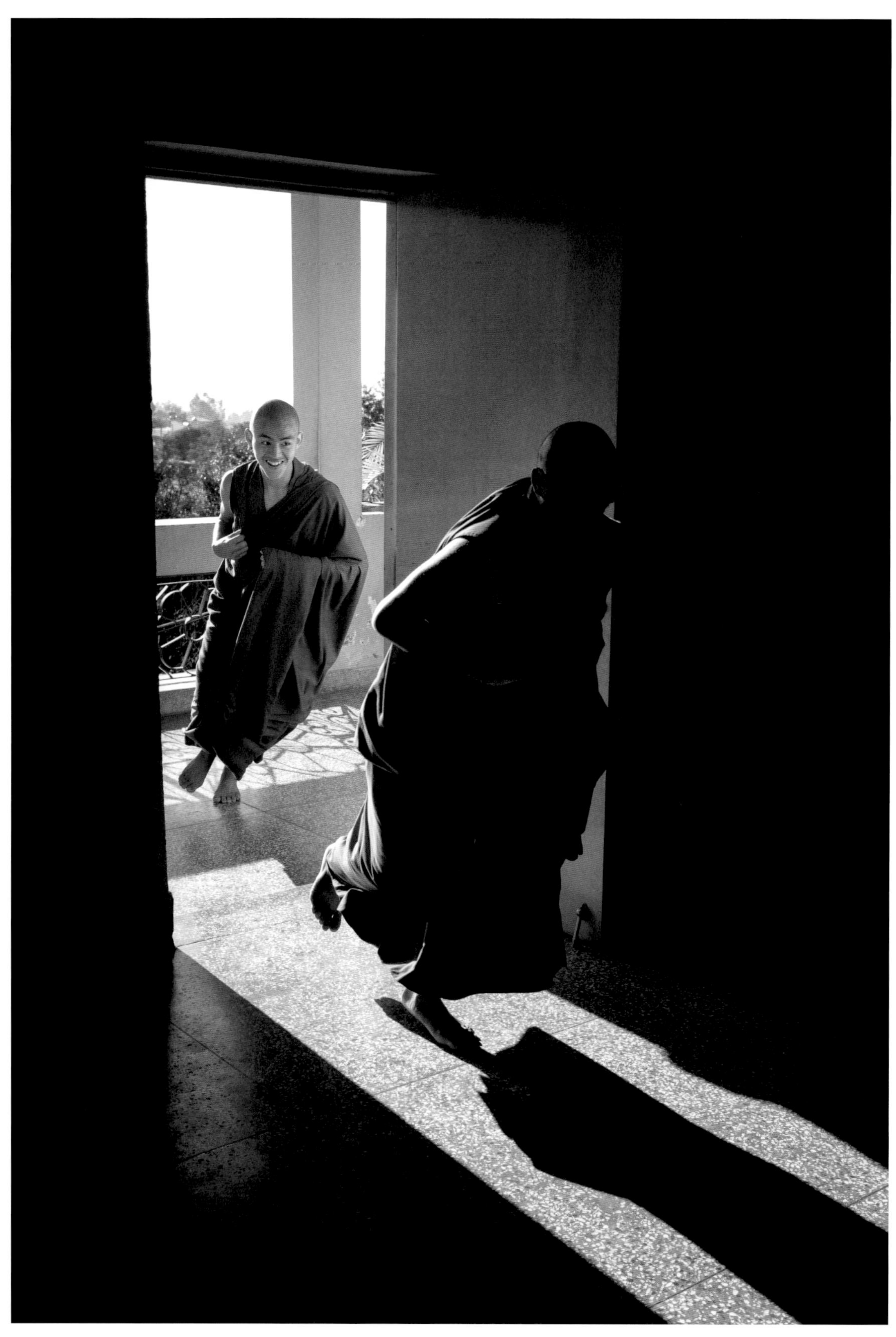

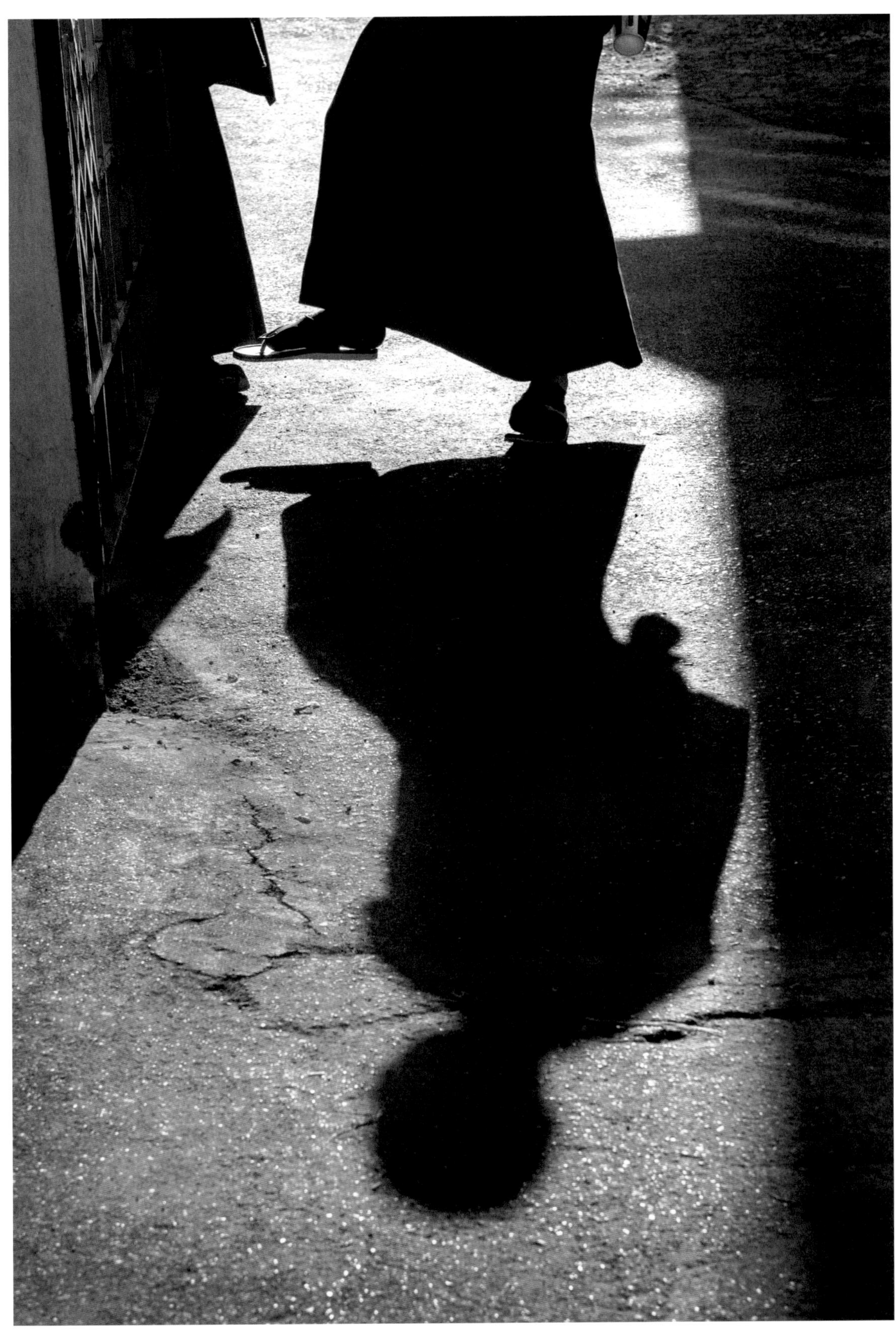

AFTERWORD

These images and words can not speak for a lifetime in the Gyuto Monastery, that would be impossible for me as a Westerner and spiritual outsider.

Generously the monks opened the doors of their monastery allowing me to see and experience this world of ancient rituals and daily commitments. The monastery is as much a state of mind as it is an architectural fact .

Their monastic life is a commitment to making their human life count. They are ordinary men who have made an extraordinarily difficult life choice. And it is hard. Many drop out in the early stages, more than 90% leave, some even after 20 or 30 years in the monastery.

Life at the monastery is one of repetition of rituals, texts and chants. The Gyuto Monastery's rituals are unchanged for centuries even as the world moves around them. The monks are not immune to 21st century temptations, mobile phones being as much a part of their lives as they are of ours.

In the Buddhist way, there is no past and no future, just the present moment. Each moment passed in the monastery is a contradiction of the impermanence of life against the continuity of tradition - an unbroken one spanning over 600 years.

Tobi Wilkinson

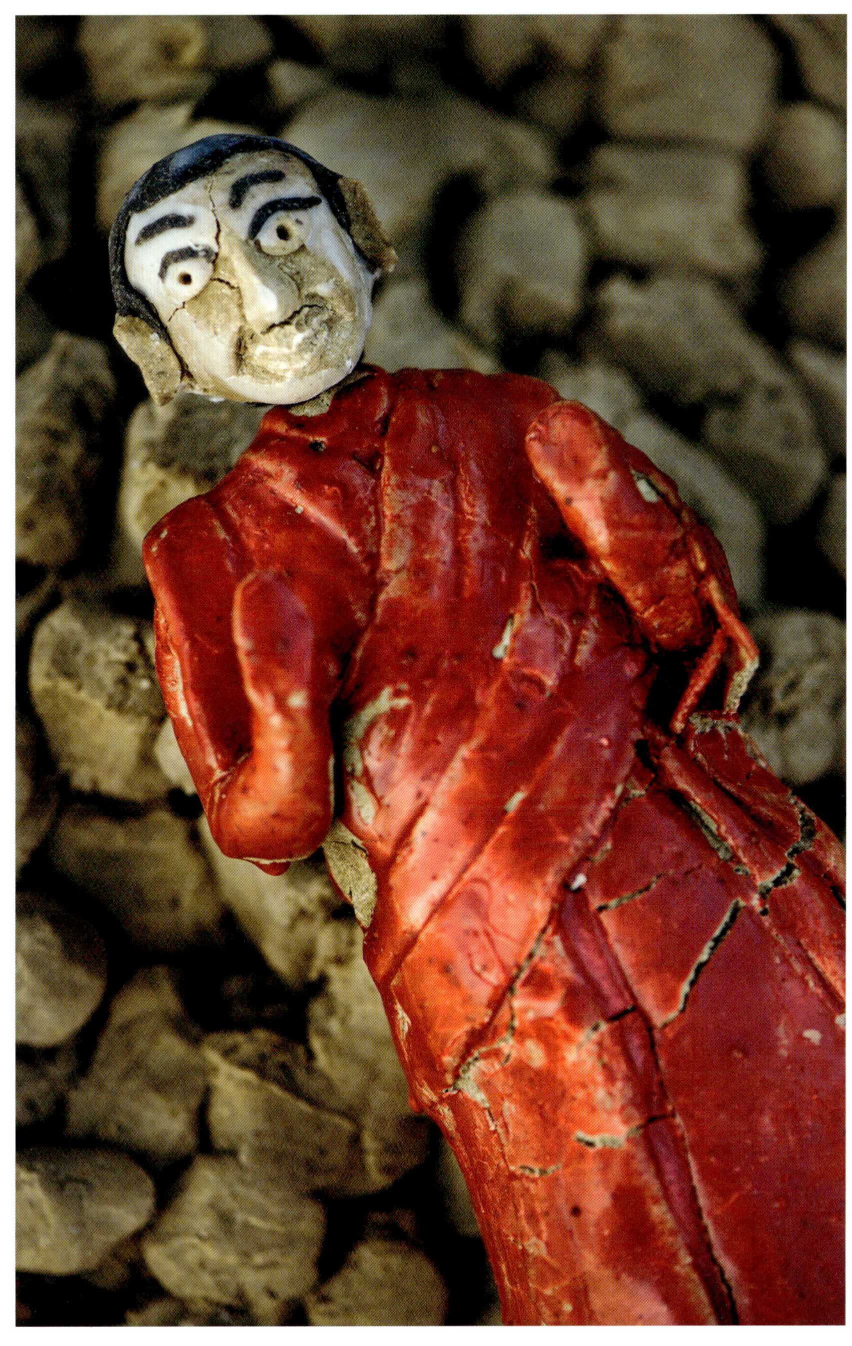

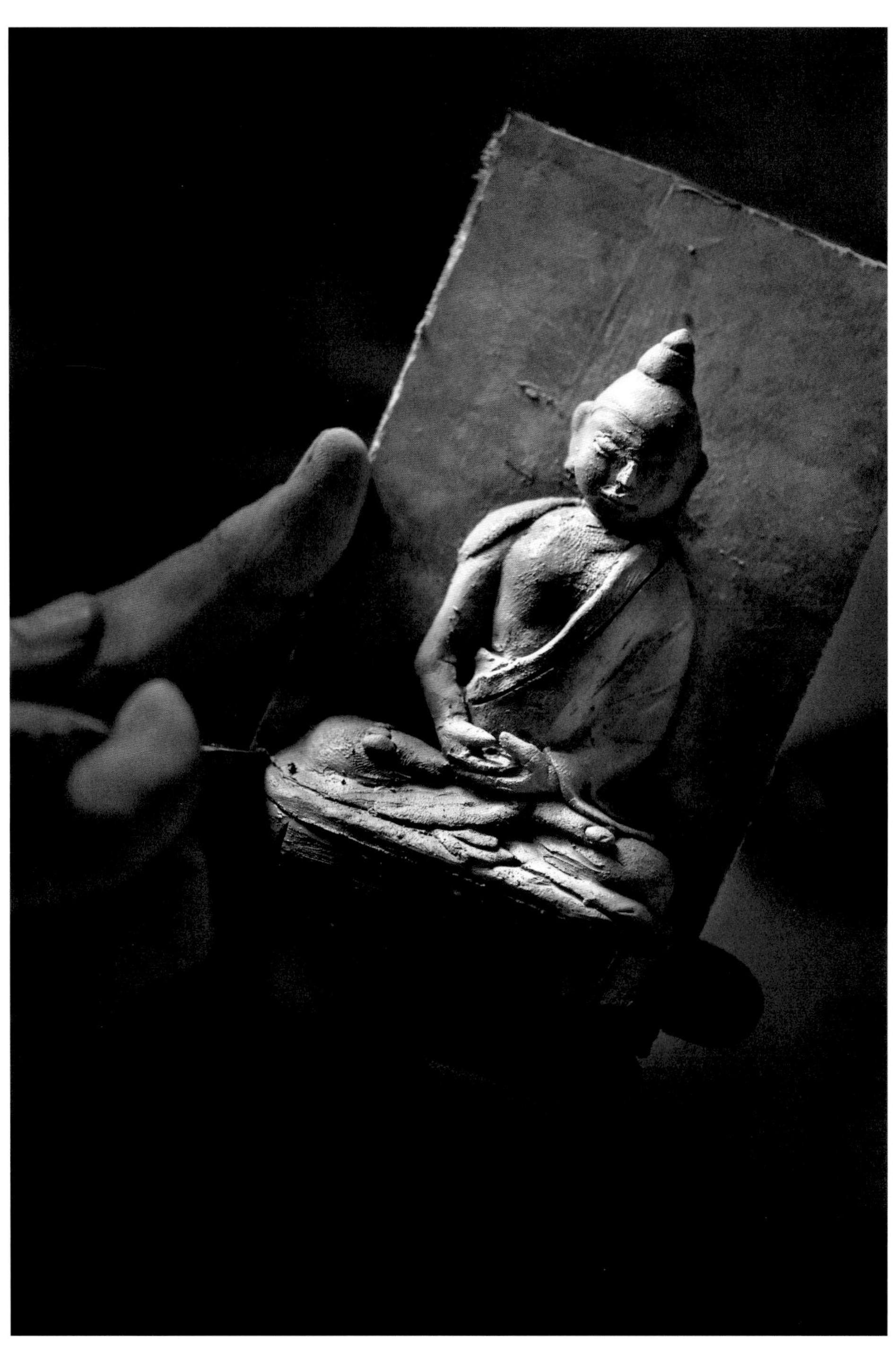

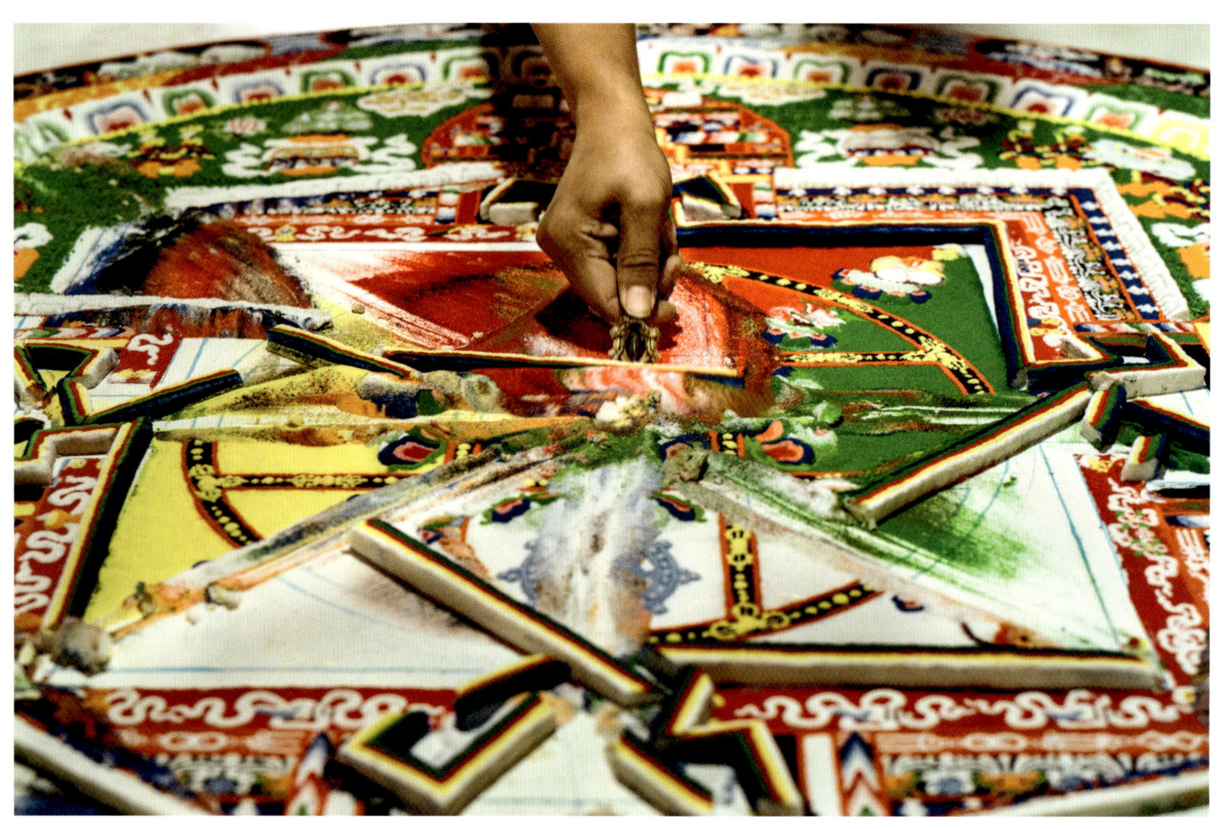

Dissolve the fear of dying to live well.

Impermanence.

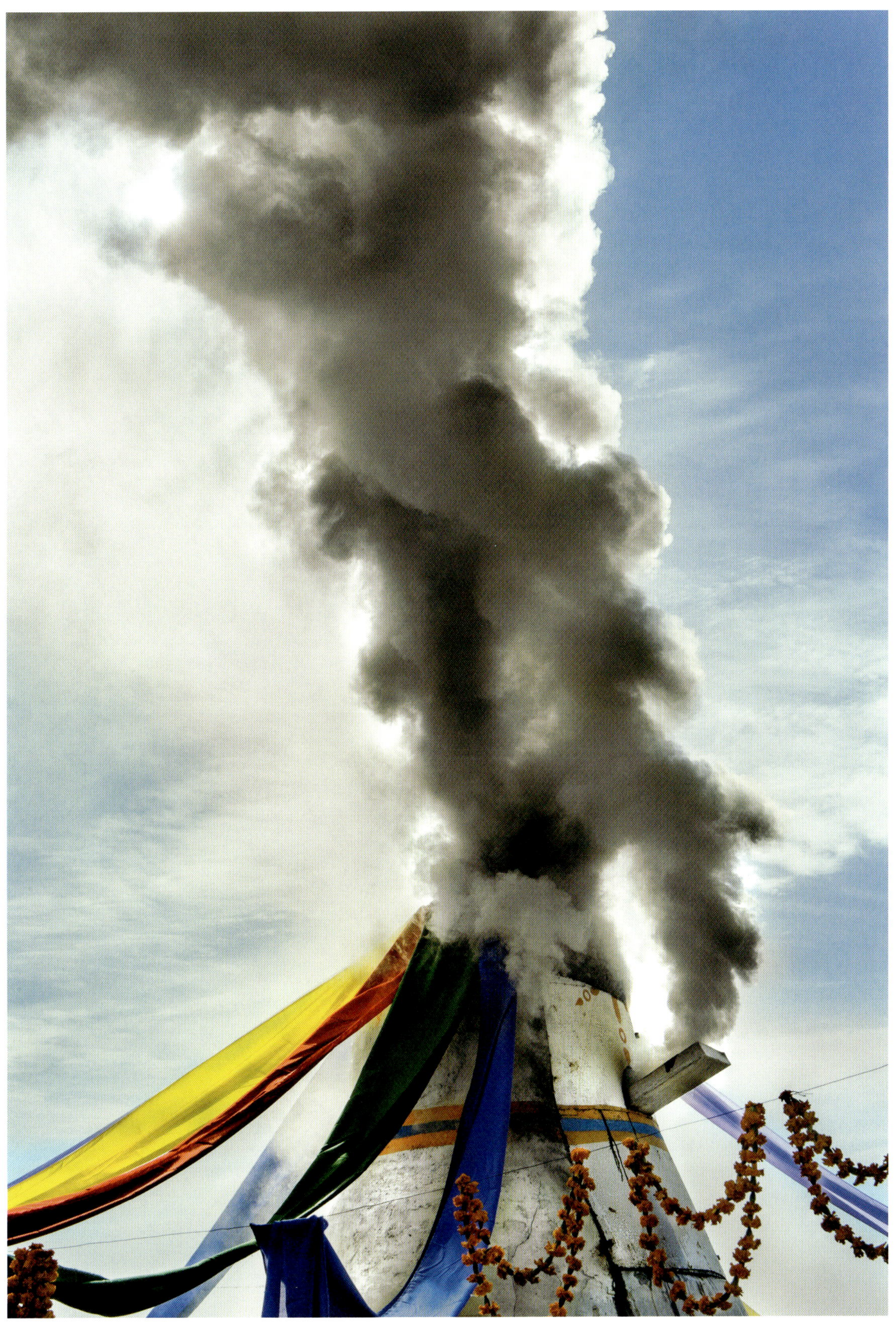